Because of the
ANGER,
I Almost Lost
EVERYTHING

Because of the ANGER, I Almost Lost EVERYTHING

Free Yourself from the Torment of Anger

MARIO FERRO

Edition: Nancy Pineda

Library of Congress Control Number:		2018906406
ISBN:	Hardcover	978-1-5065-2469-6
	Softcover	978-1-5065-2467-2
	Ebook	978-1-5065-2468-9

Print information available on the last page.

Rev. date: 09/13/2018

To order additional copies of this book, contact:
Palibrio
1663 Liberty Drive
Suite 200
Bloomington, IN 47403
Toll Free from the U.S.A 877.407.5847
Toll Free from Mexico 01.800.288.2243
Toll Free from Spain 900.866.949
From other International locations +1.812.671.9757
Fax: 01.812.355.1576
orders@palibrio.com
776198

CONTENTS

DEDICATION

T O NELLY, MY beloved wife, who brings me so much. My love, I hope that the Lord gives us a dwelling together in Heaven, because meeting you and living by your side has been spectacular. Nelly, you have made me laugh and taught me how to love life. You never abandoned me and have always believed in me. Not only did you introduce me to our Savior, but you also accompanied me throughout the process of my transformation. Your love has helped me grow and change. Every day I am more in love with you.

To my three children, Daniela, David, and Camila, that have supported me in this journey and have seen me with eyes of faith. The three of you are a miracle, I love you!

ACKNOWLEDGEMENTS

T O MY SISTER, my companion on this spectacular journey, you have helped me with your love and comprehension. A brave, hardworking woman who is adventurous and self-sacrificing, as well as being an exemplary and devoted mother. Her children are a blessing to me.

To Iván, for your encouragement, you helped me enjoy the writing process of this project that is so close to my heart. Each time you reviewed the drafts they improved as a result of your sense of humor.

To Elizabeth, whose spirituality and guidance were key in those moments when I didn't know where to start.

To the team of men and women who have walked with me in the ministry and have been devoted for so many years. They have known the Mario from both before and after the change. They know who they are and how much I love them. Thank you for putting up with me.

To Nadeyda, for your valuable contributions.

To the WWJD churches, which have been the incentive to continue walking with Jesus daily.

To the pastors who have helped me in shepherding our churches.

To the leaders of WWJD, men and women who have given up their lives to serve their disciples.

To each of the beautiful little lambs that God has allowed me to shepherd.

And my greatest appreciation is towards God, who has given me the strength to complete this project. Glory be to Him!

PROLOGUE

A *DEMON DID It* is a book that will be of great value for every person, whether to help themselves or to help others. As you read it you will receive explanations that will allow you to better understand yourself and those around you.

This book is about the process Mario Ferro, my husband, endured as God guided us through the process of facing his anger problem and learning to manage it. Moreover, you will also enjoy a dramatic, but charming story, since it is a beautiful thing to see how God works in the lives of human beings. The Mario that God allowed me to see in the beginning of our marriage was a beautiful man with a generous, loving, and caring heart. However, the anger coming from his wariness of being hurt and the threat of a possible loss, led him to control through fear. All of this made him a horrible person who nobody wanted to be with.

****

Sometimes I began to pray, devastated, but I came out on the other side with faith and full of hope.

****

The role of the affected person's companion is extremely important. I would like to say it was easy, but his change did not happen overnight. I believe that the key was to keep praying, sheltering myself and letting off steam every day with my Lord. Sometimes when I began to pray I felt hopeless, but once I finished I was renewed, full of faith and hope. This is exactly what I passed on to Mario, because Mario had absolutely no faith in his own change.

When we think about it, we realize that this book not only teaches us about ourselves, but also about our enemy's plans to destroy us. Our enemy has always tried to hurt us, our parents and our children, by creating, in the most astute possible way, a chain of destruction and death. If you manage to see this in your own life, it will be the beginning of a change.

In Mario's case it was anger, but in the same way, alcoholism, drugs, depression, constant frustrations, chronic bitterness, as well as any other restraints, be they sexual or of any other type, originate in our past. If they are not resolved, bitterness and blame cause tremendous damage in a person's life. This story will allow you to see that.

We have to fight for what God has already given us. We have the right to be happy, to live new lives. That is what Jesus achieved on the cross. Our Father's wish is for us to prosper in every aspect of our life. I hope you enjoy this book as much as I did and are successful in everything you do, with the help of the Holy Spirit. Your Father loves you... and remember that "you can do anything through Christ!"

Nelly Moreno

INTRODUCTION

B Y THE GRACE of God, today I am the pastor of a beautiful and prosperous Christian Church in southern Florida. I have a beautiful home, three children who I love, a son-in-law, and a granddaughter who, when she comes to visit, doesn't let me sleep.

At first sight, this probably doesn't seem strange but, dear reader, as you continue reading the testimony you have in your hands, you will understand that it is nothing short of a miracle. In reality, it is God's work that has allowed all these people to continue by my side. I was "predestined" to lose them all and to end up bitter and alone.

****

I was "predestined" to lose them all and to end up bitter and alone.

****

I have to admit that I did not expect this to be my first book. I desired to write about more honorable subjects that would present me in a better image. However through my daily work as a pastor, I began to understand that I serve God and His church before myself. Instead of trying to explain theological concepts or the spiritual battles taking place in the world, I had to start off by telling my story. I began to understand the need to share my testimony of how to face up to the enemy that was determined to destroy my life and my family.

Like all humans, it is clear that I was not born as a pastor, a father, a husband and much less a grandfather.

This book will not give you the answers to such complex issues. These pages contain the expression of a need to tell you about something that is silently at work and destroys homes even more than infidelity and addiction... I am talking about anger!

As most people, I got married to be happy and had the opportunity to marry the most beautiful woman I had ever met in my life. I wanted her life to be filled with joy, to smother her with love, ideally I wanted to live the fairy tale life we're all told about as children, but that very few people have been able to experience in real life.

****

As most people, I got married to be happy and had the opportunity to marry the most beautiful woman I had ever met in my life.

****

In spite of my good intentions, the first ten years of my marriage were the closest thing to hell that my wife and children got to experience. You might think I was a terrible man, a villain with a face marked by bitterness, but in reality most people viewed me as a prosperous person, a normal believer who regularly attended church and started to get involved in the ministry.

If I was prosperous, I had married the love of my life, and I had found Jesus Christ, why did my family live in fear? The answer was simple as well as painful: because of anger. Because of that uncontrollable rage that many people feel and cannot dominate; because of that violence that arises naturally in the middle of a conversation; because of the fury of the shouting without any apparent reason; because of the inability to be happy, although it is what you deeply desire; because of the destroyed nerves of your loved ones; because of the wrath that floods out when things don't go your way; because you cannot accept how mistaken you are and react terribly before the smallest observations. In a nutshell, because my life was full of acts of violence which followed a sequence like the script of a soap opera full of shouting, overreactions and always ending with the same conclusion: moments filled with shame and regret which lasted until I was "annoyed" again.

Are you an angry person, or do you know one? Do you know a person who acts perfectly in society and goes unnoticed, but whose family reflects the fear and anguish that they are living when no-one is looking? The truth is one thing is what we see in the street, at work, at school and even in church versus what is seen behind closed doors. It turns out that most of the times it is a completely different story.

****

The truth is one thing is what we see in the street, at work, at school and even in church versus what is seen behind closed doors. It turns out that most of the times it is a completely different story.

****

Is it possible to find that we are living another person's life? Could something like a spiritual inheritance exist, that passes from one generation to the next, affecting the lives of entire families for centuries? When I began to analyze my own life, I came to the conclusion that such a thing is possible. However, how can I end up repeating my father's mistakes? How could I end up doing exactly what I saw as a child and swore I would never do? How can I face the same obstacles as my father and my grandfather?

Many of us think we have escaped our family's past because we don't have the same flaws as our grandparents or parents, but what we don't realize is that there's more to it than just our genetic makeup. The bad habits, the fear we feel or instill in others are also affects our lives and acts as a curse. It is something that is there, but that you can't touch, that you can't identify at first sight and that needs a certain degree of discernment in order to see it.

As a believer in God and in the spiritual world, I have found the answers and I have been able to help myself by trusting in the Word of God. However, what about the millions and millions of human beings that can't see it? Many believers are still victims of these entities of evil that prevent them from enjoying the freedom that God has given us, His children, and live mediocre lives lacking in happiness and peace.

****

This book is my personal testimony of how I passed through the valley of death and felt the divine protection and care of God that never abandoned me.

****

For this reason, I believe it is my duty to tell my own story. So the time has arrived for me to tell each and every one of you how my children are free, as far as I can tell, of those powers that affected my grandfather, my father and myself. This book is my personal testimony of how I passed through the valley of death and felt the divine protection and care of God that never abandoned me. Surely this is the weapon that evil host's use to keep people chained up and take away power from God's children.

Believe me, demons are at work and they are more active than both people and the Church want to admit. The man telling you this was once a sceptic, but faced with the weight of proof, I could not do anything else but learn from my mistakes. This book is about how a Christian pastor was able to be liberated from rage.

1

A Complicated Birth

IN THE OPINION of several of my parent's family members, my birth was something that should have never happened. With a diabetic mother and four siblings that died at birth, the odds of my birth were not favorable. Luckily, our arrival into this world is not based on probabilities like the casinos in Las Vegas, but rather on purposes and I had a very important one in my path.

My mother was born into a family where surnames, a good reputation and the ownership of large areas of land were very important. My father, on the other hand, came from a middle class family from southern Colombia. Due to her diabetes, my mother was a spoiled child who got everything she wanted without any resistance from my grandparents.

And Love Arrived...

My parents met during a regional festival and it was love at first sight. Shortly after meeting, they got married in order to start a family. In spite of the opposition they were facing from my mother's family which only made her desperately cling to this relationship. Overcoming all the obstacles in their way, my parents arrived in the country's capital and started their new life from zero.

Thanks to the connections of my mother's family, my father got an excellent job in the country's issuing bank and soon worked his way up the ranks. Through effort and sacrifice, he finished his studies and became a professional, giving my mother everything she was used to as a child. In the end, due to his high intelligence quotient, my father quite easily advanced both socially and culturally.

If my father had all these qualities, why did my mother's family oppose this relationship that made her so happy? Was it simple selfishness or had they seen something that my young mother didn't? Of course, it was the latter, since they could clearly see my father's character with his irascible and explosive temperament. My mother thought that they could overcome it, and with her eyes closed, she began her marriage to a man with a volatile character.

****

What she saw in her partner, in the love of her life, was a wonderful man, an artist, a mathematician, a musician, an odonatologist, a karateka, a sculptor, a sportsman, a painter, a cabinet maker, a carpenter and a business man.

****

What she saw in her partner, in the love of her life, was a wonderful man, an artist, a mathematician, a musician, an odonatologist, a karateka, a sculptor, a sportsman, a painter, a cabinet maker, a carpenter and a business man. You might think I am exaggerating, but I have met only few people in my lifetime that have similar virtuous characteristics. A person who is so in love with the arts while simultaneously being a genius.

A Sad Reality

Without a doubt, my father had many qualities, but his defects, which were only two, annulled everything else. His bad temper and his love for drinking were an extremely dangerous mix, so much so that it completely changed the lives of those of us who loved him. Once he started drinking liquor he could last for a week. So the parties in my house were always long and exhausting.

Any time my father started a celebration, my mother hid the most expensive vases and any porcelain because she knew there would be problems. In fact, when he got too drunk, the situation could change in a matter of seconds. Just a gesture, a lack of food or alcohol, someone wanting to go out but my father not agreeing, was enough to start the shouting, hitting and kicking. Even today, I don't know how we avoided a tragedy because of the high level of violence in our house.

Because of these characteristics which my father demonstrated since he was young, my mother's family tried to oppose their daughter's wishes. If they had never denied her anything, how could they make her reconsider and accept a "no" as an answer? Consequently, her family couldn't do anything about it and she married the love of her life.

My Arrival Into the World

Due to her illness, my mother had four miscarriages before having my big sister. Then, once this miracle had happened, my father longed for a son and my mother, wanted to please him thinking that maybe it would improve their troubled marriage. I was born on August 4th, with heart problems and underdeveloped lungs. I came into this world prematurely and without asking permission, just to make my mother happy.

I was born in the most complicated month of a pregnancy, the eighth, when my mother was suffering from a blood sugar level crisis. My heart was too small and I weighed so little that they did not think I would survive. As you can see, I came into this world with more problems than solutions.

****

As you can see, I came into this world with more problems than solutions.

****

Due to my heart problems, the color of my skin was quite strange. I spent the first few months of my life in an incubator and the odds were stacked against me. Despite this, against all odds, I kept growing. Since I came into this world, life was telling me it wasn't going to be easy. This is why, without realizing it, every test for survival turned me into a fighter. I hung onto my existence in such a way that it became a point of conversation among my family and my mother made sure to remind me of the value of each day that I managed to survive in the hospital's intensive care room.

We don't all start life in the same way, but it is a fact that some day we will ask ourselves, "What am I doing here?" That is exactly what I asked myself one day, since after so many exhausting endeavors at such a young age, life seemed quite tragic to me. I thought that I was not special in any way and that my life required a lot of effort. Why did I come into this world? That was the question!

After so many difficult moments, there were times in my life that I just didn't have enough strength. Maybe you have felt the same way, but I found a word in the Bible during one of my worst moments and it became one of the fundamental revelations in my life. It was in Psalm 139, that I read that God created my body in my mother's womb, that He looked at my embryo and that He planned out everything in my life. In that moment I understood that my life had a purpose…and yours does too!

2

A Dysfunctional Childhood

E VEN TODAY, I still remember a glass ashtray smashing into a thousand pieces against the dining room wall, just because someone dared to contradict my father. When he arrived home after work, my sister, my mother and I wanted to hide or leave, but we couldn't. Instead, we had to smile and greet him with a kiss on the cheek, regardless of his attitude. Then, he washed his hands and my mother served dinner. My father ate without saying a word and no-one spoke. We ate in total silence. When he finished eating, he banged his plate a few times with his fork and this was the sign for me to clear the table while he went to watch some television before going to bed. That was when we could relax a bit, obviously without making any noise, so that we didn't wake him up.

****

I remember that sometimes the nerves of not being able to make any noise made my sister and I laugh incessantly.

****

I remember that sometimes the nerves of not being able to make any noise made my sister and I laugh incessantly, so we had to cover our mouths to stop our mother suffering. Then… to bed in silence!

Mornings were the same: a quick breakfast in tension because my father listened to the sad songs, boleros or ballads on the radiogram (for the new generations this would be the equivalent to an iPod or any other device for listening to music) while he shaved.

That was our daily routine while my mother prepared our lunches and brought us to the school bus, where she faced another of her greatest fears: losing us. My mother overprotected us from everything and everyone. On many occasions, we didn't even get on the bus, because she was so worried about leaving us by ourselves when we were so small. So, whether we went to school or not depended on my mother's mood. This all happened behind my father's back because, for him, school and studying were very important. So much, that once, when I was six years old and he found out that I still didn't know how to read, he told me that if I didn't know how to read and write by the next day he would hit me with a whip he had specially made.

I should clarify that, although I learned to read and write in twenty-four hours, my father still found a day to use his much loved method of physical punishment. That day he and my mother had a huge argument. She was seriously harmed after receiving the whipping that was meant to be for me. That moment is still fresh in my mind. I remember that the furious whip was coming straight towards my face and there was nothing I could do to prevent it, my face would be scarred for life. Suddenly time stopped or maybe it just started going slower, I'm not sure, but I can remember every detail of the whole event.

Educating or "Uneducating"?

In those days, I was like any other six year old, quite fidgety, but it seemed that my father's nervous system couldn't cope with this. So he decided it was time to start educating me and came to the conclusion that the best way to do this was using the same method that had been used with him. This resulted in him making a whip out of leather and the cable from the electric iron.

The scenario was ready and the emotions were at the highest. It was like I was the accused against whom the proof had been building up throughout the trial until the day of sentencing.

Finally, the day arrived for my father to try out his new method of punishment. He wasn't in the mood to put up with any more of my foolishness. That day I did something that annoyed him so much that, without thinking twice, he went to the closet where he hid his "character reformer" and, without saying a word, just a dry shout, he lifted his arm and, with fury, directed all the anger and annoyance within him on the face of a small six-year old boy.

I couldn't do anything to escape and there was no more time for begging. He caught me by surprise and was in front of me before I could avoid him. The punishment, the cable and the leather came through the air in a macabre dance, almost laughing at me, because they had come together for this moment.

My father' once artistic hands now caressed the whipping material over and over, weaving them in such a way that my disobedience would receive an efficient punishment. They would be merciless, fulfilling their purpose on me, to teach me. Yes, "To teach me". That was the phrase he repeated to himself as he was interweaving them. Also, so that I would remember, but what would they make me remember? What lesson did my father want to teach me? Well, the leather and the cable didn't know. However, when frustration, bitterness and rage flow through a human being's sweat, they christen everything with hate and can only cause evil and destruction in their path.

****

I could almost see them smiling at me, as they came closer, ready to impose the punishment for my childlike actions.

****

I could almost see them smiling at me, as they came closer, ready to impose the punishment for my childlike actions. Then a miracle happened. In an instant, something stopped them in their path, completely diverting them from their main target: my face. The blood flowed from an injury that happened right in front of my eyes. My mother's leg was like a protecting shield that crossed the path of my father's discipline.

I can still hear her words in my head: "Not him. Do whatever you want to me, but leave the child alone", shouted my mother. Maybe his shame or seeing the state of my mother's leg, made him curse and leave. There was no pause to bandage the wound, to apologize or to try and understand the irrational situation. Just an insult and he left. The two of us stayed there in silence. There were no words, although the truth is that at the time words weren't needed. My mother's eyes showed what she was ready to suffer for me.

A Love I Couldn't Understand

With these events occurring since my early years, the idea of a fair God was blurred in my heart. I was told many times about God, Jesus of Nazareth, that loved me and had always been there waiting for me. Those words sounded empty and meaningless. How could a loving God have allowed my poor mother to suffer that punishment that was destined for me?

Sixteen years later, in the middle of a life that couldn't find its way, this past event became so big for me that I understood why that God, who was passionate and loving, allowed me to go through this dark and horrible moment. To feel loved by God is a miracle, to feel forgiven is even greater, but to understand that God has always been there, that Jesus has been beside you every step of the way, is the most healing experience that anyone can live on this earth.

To feel loved by God is a miracle, to feel forgiven is even greater, but to understand that God has always been there, that Jesus has been beside you every step of the way, is the most healing experience that anyone can live on this earth.

As an adult, I went to church, listened to the sermons, heard good advice, learned the hymns and even read the Bible. Meanwhile, deep inside me, I knew that I could not feel the heavenly Father's love that many people talked about, without really believing in it. How could I believe? How could I have faith in Christ? How could I understand the Father's love offered to me by God? How could I forgive? How could I, maybe, forget?

A Supernatural Experience

Suddenly, one day, in the middle of my confusion (don't ask me how), I saw him... I saw Jesus being flagellated and suffering every lash, like snakes' tongues, destroying His beautiful skin. I saw him there, humiliated, receiving the punishment without being guilty of anything. A glorious and eternal echo through time came to my life at that precious moment.

That whip, those hands, the air filled with anger, two scenarios that were both different and so similar at the same time... and I was in both of them! It was me in my house at almost six years old, the whip, the fury and my mother's leg in the middle. Two thousand years before and after, we were the whip, the body, the beautiful skin of my Lord Jesus in the middle and me. God was talking to me and His Word was finally making sense. The Bible says that the punishment for our rebellions was paid by Him, that we were cured by Christ's wounds and that He became cursed so that the curses did not fall on God's children.

For years, I couldn't feel Jesus close to me, and every time people talked to me about the love of God, deep inside I was laughing to myself. Meanwhile, the truth was in front of me, clear, transparent and diaphanous: my mother's love was like God's love. She was prepared to put herself between the anger of my father and my face, and Jesus followed the Father's orders to put Himself between my deserved punishment and myself.

Think of a personal experience in which someone helped you, in which someone, without knowing why, paid something for you. This is a strange occurrence in a world full of selfishness and materialism, but God uses human beings and circumstances to manifest Himself to his children in a way that no-one can deny.

****

God uses human beings and circumstances to manifest Himself to his children in a way that no-one can deny.

****

The Reality of God's Love

What I am trying to say here is that you need to feel loved by God, forgiven and free. If you cannot feel God's love, it will not be possible for you to love others. Today is the day. It is not a coincidence that you and I are "talking" about this matter. Kneel down wherever you are and ask God for a sign, a revelation of his genuine love. If you have been treated badly, humiliated or abused, or if on the contrary, you have done so to others, you need to receive this miraculous gift right now.

MARIO FERRO

Forgive and be forgiven... that is the key! However, without heaven's permission, it is impossible for a human being to really do this. Call to God and don't give up. Fill the skies with your prayers until you receive an answer and always remember that the punishment was meant for you. You should also remember that Jesus has been walking by your side daily, even though you haven't noticed.

3

A Scarred Memory

ON THIS JOURNEY through the episodes that marked my childhood, there is another moment which left an impression on me. My father, Gerardo's shirt was ripped, bloody and open because of the few buttons left on it. His dark brown wavy hair was messy and completely flattened with a mixture of sweat and blood. He was lying on the bunkbed of a cell and when he saw us, he threw himself at the bars that were keeping him in and started saying things that I have already forgotten.

Gloria, my mother, looked at him, astonished, but resigned, in a somewhat familiar scene. It was three o'clock in the morning in a city where darkness is the perfect hideout for muggers and unsavory characters. There we were, my sister, who is two years older than me, my mother, my father, on the other side of the bars asking to get out, and me. The whole family was together in that horrible place for something that half of us didn't understand.

Everything began when my mom woke us in the middle of the night and got us dressed. She told us that we had to go with her because she couldn't leave us home alone and she didn't have anyone else to come and look after us. So we went out into the darkness to get a taxi. We walked through the deserted and dangerous streets. Gloria was a housewife who was not used to this kind of situation. Despite this, she got us ready to go out on a Friday night, almost Saturday at dawn, taking a kitchen knife with her for protection under her black coat.

Now I don't think she would have been capable of using it, but I imagine that it would have made her feel better. We finally arrived at the police station full of vagrants, police officers and drunks, where my father, who was still quite drunk, talked to us through the bars. My mother paid the bail and they let us take him home with us in the same taxi that was waiting for us outside.

****

God uses human beings and circumstances to manifest himself to his children in a way that no-one can deny.

****

That night my mom explained to us that my father went to a party with one of his best friends, and after several drinks, they got into a fight and that his friend ended up in the cell next to his. It seems that it was quite a serious fight. My father's body had lots of scratches, wounds and bruises, as well as blood all over his face and part of his clothes. I thought that it was ugly, unpleasant, and pathetic this was all foreign to me.

The Same Scene with Other Protagonists

I would never have imagined that about fifteen years later, I would be in a similar situation! There I was in a provisional cell in a detention area in the middle of the street waiting to be driven to a jail for attacking a man in the parking lot of a mall. It all began when a stranger attacked me after I had frightened him by speeding through the parking lot.

The stranger put his head through the driver's window and started hitting me while shouting furiously. Little did the poor man know that his fury was nothing in comparison to my fury. I hit back in self-defense, but I battered him so badly that when the police arrived, I had changed from being the victim to the attacker.

According to the police officers who arrived on the scene, whereas the other man had various injuries, I had almost none and it was his word against mine. So, it was up to me to prove my innocence before a judge, but first I had to spend some time in a cell. In the end, I came to an agreement with the other man, not before handing over a large sum of money to prevent my name being involved in a scandal in the press, since in those days I was a well-known television actor.

****

Maybe that scene came back to me to remind me that everything has a beginning and nothing happens by coincidence.

****

Maybe that scene came back to me to remind me that everything has a beginning and nothing happens by coincidence. My father and I ended up in similar cells at different times. How does a person end up turning into what they fear, into what they never wanted to be? The time I was arrested was just a prelude of what I would experience in later years.

4

A Christmas without gifts

M Y FATHER TOLD us that this Christmas there would be no presents. He did not allow my mother to give anything to my sister and me. There were no motives, no reasons; it was just his way of getting revenge on God for what He denied him that sad Christmas.

Christian media talks a lot about the dependence and obedience of women towards men. Christians are taught that women must unconditionally obey their husband's orders. However, I firmly believe that if my mother had done everything my father ordered her to do; neither my sister nor I would have reached adulthood.

An Unexpected Event

I remember that Christmas like it was yesterday. I was told about the birth of God and that it was a time of happiness. It was for this reason that parents give their children presents on behalf of God. I was only seven years old and the concept of God was not very clear in my mind. I just knew that He was someone good who lived in heaven and gave presents every Christmas because a little boy of His was born every December. That Christmas would be the last that we would celebrate together as a family, since the dark cloud represented by the word divorce was gathering over our house.

How much more could my mother put up with? How much more abuse from my father was she willing to accept? I'm sure she already had her answer, and if she was going to act, that was the moment.

****

At home, the incidents were getting worse and the arguments were evidence that my father was not capable of running a family.

****

At home, the incidents were getting worse and the arguments were evidence that my father was not capable of running a family. Gloria was pregnant with a little one. (The strange thing is that I don't remember her getting fat or having a tummy, I just remember her leaving for the hospital the day of the birth).

My next memory is of my father drinking and listening to music. I was told that my mother was in the hospital and that we'd soon have a new addition to the family. But, why was my dad at home? No-one told me at the time, but I later discovered that my little sister was born and died the next day. That was why my father was drinking and blaming heaven for all his misfortunes. The music was very sad. The songs were boleros by Javier Solís, music made for and inspired by moments of great anguish and desperation.

Believe me, that music did not positively contribute to the mood of someone like my father who, at that time, needed words of encouragement, not words from someone who died at thirty-four years old, who was famous for singing songs like: "Nothing More Than Shadows" ("Sombras Nada Más") and "I am a Sad Clown" ("Soy un Triste Payaso"). The music was at full blast, the stereo couldn't have been louder and the bottle was emptying quickly, but it didn't matter. On the shelf where that bottle came from, there were plenty more ready to drown the sorrows of someone who really believed that he was the saddest person in the world that day. Someone wanted to silence their sadness at all costs and that person was my father. In spite of everything, my love and admiration for him were unparalleled.

When my father wasn't drinking, he was very special. He was a man who was gifted with many attributes and qualities. He was a senior executive of the country's issuing bank, a man born to triumph according to everyone that knew him. Of course, they weren't there that day.

In Imminent Danger

The bottle was finished; it let its last drop escape like someone who exhales his last breath before dying. Slowly, my father walked to the bar he had built with his own hands, to look for the other bottles of *whisky*.

Since he was as a child, he was taught with blood that "men don't cry", so the tears that never fell because no-one had ever shown them the path, were the silent witnesses of something more than sadness. At that time, it was blind rage, anger fueled by the alcoholic haze mixed with the memories of a tragic life, like a volcano before eruption. When the eruption arrived, the tempest, the meaningless explosion, I was in the path of the disaster and it was unstoppable.

****

When the eruption arrived, the tempest, the meaningless explosion, I was in the path of the disaster and it was unstoppable.

****

Maybe I was breathing louder than I should or I was walking without taking my shoes off. I still don't know today, but he noticed I was there. He turned towards me and at that moment, I knew I had to escape, flee… but where could I hide from someone so big and strong? What wall could put space between someone who could end my life with one blow? I ran away! I think it was my survival instinct, the same one that God gave us to keep us alive when we are in danger.

My father came after me, took something off the table, I hardly saw what it was but its shine froze my blood. But, if, until now, he had never once cut me, what was I afraid of? How did I know that that instrument which was already tasting my skin could hurt me? Well, there wasn't much time to think about it. It was a matter of survival. Until when? It didn't matter, each instant was life and life should be protected. That's what my brain kept telling me. I got to the master bedroom... and my mother? Where was my divine shield? Where was the person who protected me at times like this?

My back was against the head of the bed and I made myself as small as my muscles allowed me, but he was walking quickly towards me. Everything happened quickly, like a macabre choreograph that had been planned months in advance. The sharp blade came towards me and as if in a spasm, I put a cushion between it and me. Once again, something else received the blow rather than me. I got out in one piece, without a scratch. As I ran towards the door, I saw my father lying on the bed. It looked like he was thinking about what he was about to do to his only seven year old son.

I ran through the house, got to the door and there she was, my angel, heaven's caress. My body took her form and I hugged her as if I wished I had never come into this world and was still in her stomach, where I never knew loneliness or sadness.

Her smile gave me back the breath I had lost running away. She looked me in the eyes and swore to me that everything was OK and things were going to get better. She had left the hospital against the doctor's advice. She risked her own life because she knew that, at home, two very small lives were in danger of being wiped out without her help, the two people she loved most on this earth. The incident ended there, just in my memory, but she knew... I know she knew without me having told her.

MARIO FERRO

Remembering a Smile

Against my father's wishes, there were presents that Christmas! Hidden in a closet were "Baby Angelino" and the most beautiful motorbike I had ever seen. The bows and wrapping paper showed me that the baby Jesus had been born and that happiness was everywhere. Despite this, why was my mother crying? Well, that day, she had to bury my newly-born sister as well as any hopes of ever saving her marriage.

Looking back on that day, I remember my mother's smile and hug and noticing they were not normal. Today, I can feel the love of God comforting me through my mother, the love that God has put in almost all mothers as a reflection of His presence in our lives. Her smile continues to heal me even though it is no longer with me. That smile reminds me of how God has loved me from the beginning. God is the one is responsible for saving me that day and bringing me here to you to tell you that He wants to heal you and give you the opportunity of a new life. Try to remember that smile from someone in your past, the tender hug that comforted you, the word that soothed you like healing oil, He was there.

****

Try to remember that smile from someone in your past, the tender hug that comforted you, the word that soothed you like healing oil, He was there.

****

God allowed that tenderness to act as a sign of His love. The love of God is the love that heals. Our good Father's love and tenderness is what guides others to bless us with His presence. Do not be fooled by those who say that "they made it by themselves" and that no-one helped them. There has always been a hand leading us along the way. Amnesia is not good when it is related to gratitude. Think of that smile, of that caress and feel the reflection of God present in your life!

5

The Separation

FOR OUR FATHER, economic provision was a priority. In other words, our home's cupboard and refrigerator had to be full because it served as a sign of economic prosperity and wellbeing. In that moment he wouldn't have imagined that his marriage was falling apart with a wife who grew more ill by the day and with children who were extremely traumatized.

My mother looked for all types of help for both herself and her children. Her nerves were gradually deteriorating and she began to take medication prescribed by her psychiatrist. I saw her taking entire boxes of those pills as if they were candies. It reached the point that it was not just one, but several pills per day.

The boxes were emptying quickly. Then she would desperately call the doctor because, in her opinion, the pills were not working. As a result, the pills were changed for stronger ones. My mother ended up addicted to tranquilizers. She knew that she could not put up with so much anxiety on her own. She needed something to help her remain calm when faced with my father's fury.

****

My mother ended up addicted to tranquilizers. She knew that she could not put up with so much anxiety on her own. She needed something to help her remain calm when faced with my father's fury.

****

Now, my mother's dependency on tranquilizer pills was growing. We went from doctors' home visits to long and boring waits in doctors' offices, strange places where adults sat for hours pretending that they didn't need any help. In these places, the waiting rooms normally had a big photo of a nurse with a finger to her lips asking for silence and music that was meant to be calming, but in reality the music made the atmosphere of the room feel gloomy. My mother started to repeat the same routine so many times a week that I began to think that my mother's hobby was to sit in a waiting room.

An Unexpected Turn of Events

One day everything changed. I remember leaving my mother in the waiting room, with the excuse of going to the restroom. Out of curiosity I went into a conference that was being given at the same place. I sat in the last row and, as it happened, I began to understand what the doctor was talking about. He was clearly describing my mother's illness and I understood everything. It was incurable. His words also led me to believe that she was going to die young. It was something terrible and painful to hear. That day I knew that she didn't have much longer to live and I felt dizzy, transported to somewhere else. My mind was playing tricks with me, as if the room was expanding and shrinking in an interminable symphony.

The man finished and I got up, nearly fainting, and I walked through the corridors feeling nauseous. For the first time, I understood what it meant to die: separation, pain, missing someone and letting go of what you love most. I cried inside, with no tears, no external signs, just feeling the emptiness of a future without my mother. When I saw her, I couldn't even give her a hug. She was like a stranger to me, like someone who wants to leave and cause pain. In a way, I started to protect myself and something inside of me activated, immediately an invisible and undetectable wall was raised.

Something inside of me activated, immediately an invisible and undetectable wall was raised.

I had nightmares, moments of pain between the pills, needles and trips to the doctor. Life for Gloria's children was becoming very unpleasant, so much so that I had to resort to my mind and reading comics, adventure stories and picture books in order to escape reality. Although doctors have an excellent will to serve and help the majority of their patients, there is little they can do with a mind that decides to turn itself off to avoid pain.

An Inevitable Ending

My father was also getting worse and his attacks of rage were intensifying. Unprovoked shouting, abuse, and fights at any time of the day were normal in our home. Between her diabetes and her deteriorated nerves, my mom fought to remain sane for her children. However, little by little, she fell into hysteria and began adopting my father's unpleasant character. So, one day she stood up to him and he ended up throwing her down the stairs from the second floor of our house. I was watching everything from under a small table in the hallway and that was one of the scariest moments of my life.

My mother couldn't put up with it any more. It wasn't only about the physical pain he brought upon her, but his words started to dry her up inside, they started to take away her breath and the little strength she had left after her illness. My father never showed compassion or consideration for anyone else. He only felt sorry for himself, because in his world he was the only victim. The situation became unbearable because Gloria was not only a wife, but also a mother, and what her children were going through could have a greater effect on them than the absence of their father. So, she finally made the decision.

The day that we left, I imagine that my father opened the door as usual and expected everything to be normal. But, it wasn't... The house was empty! My mother and her two children had left him and had only left a note on the dining room table, telling him that it was all over between them. She begged his forgiveness, but also asked him not to look for us, which was something almost impossible to expect from my father.

His dinner must have been warm, because my mother was looking after my father right up to the last minute. She loved him, but couldn't live with him, not so much for herself and her health, but because she knew that if we continued to live there, sooner or later a misfortune would occur, and she wasn't ready to allow what she most loved in the world to suffer the consequences of her decisions. No, she had to save her children from the man she loved.

****

She loved him, but couldn't live with him, not so much for herself and her health, but because she knew that if we continued to live there, sooner or later a misfortune would occur.

****

I later found out that my father destroyed everything in his path. Then he did what he always used to do. He went to his usual liquor store, had a fight with someone in the street, left them unconscious and returned home to the sadness that was always with him. Then, he drank himself unconscious in the middle of the chaos. The next day, he called in sick to work. Like a professional detective, he looked for the truck that had helped us move. A few days later he found it and, holding a knife to the driver's throat, threatened to kill him if he didn't take him to where he had left us. The man gave us up.

We weren't there anymore because a relative had warned my mother and we fled before he got there. When he did, it was obvious he was drunk. He returned home to continue doing what he did best. Months and years of persecution by my father, leaving no stone unturned, didn't help my mother's health. To tell the truth, her nerves couldn't take it anymore and she slowly lost her health and her life.

6

The Bionic Man

"THE BIONIC MAN", or the "Six Million Dollar Man", was a United States television series that had captivated the world. It even broke viewing records in Latin America. When I was ten years old, I dreamed of having the action figure of the series that the producers had put on the market. In Colombia, this was an impossible dream.

The economy in my house was not good. I knew this because of my mother's worried face. I knew because the days of the refrigerator overflowing with food were gone and we had entered a new period of unusual shortage. My parents' separation began to wreak havoc in our lives. My father refused to pay the monthly child support agreed before the judge and said that that was the payment for our ingratitude. I still remember that some nights our uncle Manuel would bring us bread, milk or typical Colombian food: little yellow fried potato chips, the famous "rellena", which is a kind of tube filled with rice, peas and other things that I thought were delicious, but now I would not dare to eat. At the time, they were delicacies sent from above, "the food of kings," for our new situation and dysfunctional family.

The Routine of Pain

There seemed to be an unspoken agreement that my mother's family would take turns to give us food and clothes and would try to make our lives a bit more pleasant. My mother saw herself as a failure and the "nerve" pills or tranquilizers became a more common sight on her bedside table. Every day,

the wet pillows from her tears of the night before would dry
with the warmth of despair.

****

*Every day, her pillows, wet from her tears from
the night before, dried with the warmth of despair.*

****

She was a young woman, beautiful, like a beauty queen.
Her gaze was generous and compassionate. Those who knew her
loved her and, I now know, men desired her. So, why did she
feel like that? Why could she see no future for herself? We have
to situate ourselves in the year 1976. In those days, separations
were not well accepted, and much less in my mother's family
and culture.

Marriage was sacred. You did it once and forever, without
the possibility of divorce. Who could love her again? Which
sincere man would want to take on two children who were
not his? These were questions that would not be answered for
her. The only thing that kept her going was her wish to see us
grow up, to see us "move forward" and sometimes she had to
convince herself that it was enough for her. For such a romantic
woman, living without love was like a sentence that she was
faithfully serving every day.

The antidepressants were no longer as effective. So, suddenly,
the yellow packet of pills changed to green. I think the change
of color increased the concentration in milligrams. In any case,
not only did the pill's appearance change, but so did Gloria's
mood. She gradually escaped from reality, sleeping long hours
after her usual routine of pills and glass of water.

Meanwhile, I played with my sister's toys. The funny thing
was that her doll was beautiful and represented the mother;
meanwhile, my toy was a worn-out Pinocchio that represented
the father. Was this an irony of the life that we were living,

without us even realizing it? At the end of the game, my sister's doll always divorced Pinocchio and the children went into the forest to escape the long-nosed liar.

An Unexpected Present

Life went on in a monotonous silence, trying not to make noise to avoid waking a mother who didn't want to be alive. However, every Tuesday night he appeared on our black and white television. It was the series that brought the nation to a standstill. I'm talking about my hero, who helped me forget my daily life, who had taken over my dreams and thoughts and who I waited for during six days every week.

There was Lee Majors, the actor who portrayed the bionic man, also known as the six million dollar man. The man who made many people forget their reality that many times was so sad. I don't know if he was as important for my sister as he was for me, but I still remember the music, the slow motion camera that accompanied his vertiginous run, the sound effects and his archrivals, some of which were straight out of the typical American imagination. Some of them, like Sasquatch or Big Foot, made us believe there was a being that was so strong and good that we Lilliputians could feel safe in the middle of a world full of Big Foots.

****

That morning things were not looking good for my birthday. My mother gave no sign that anything special was planned and she let me think that she had forgotten such a special day.

****

That morning things were not looking good for my birthday. My mother gave no sign that anything special was planned and she let me think that she had forgotten such a special day. So, I decided to act as if I didn't care, that it didn't matter if no-one remembered me and I acted as well as I could. I don't think I did it very well, because she couldn't resist any longer, gave me a wrapped box and wished me happy birthday.

I opened it right away…and there he was! The most beautiful action figure I had ever seen. No, I wasn't dreaming. He was wearing red sportswear and you could move the skin to see the cables that made him so strong. He also had a bionic arm just like on television. I wasn't dreaming. It was the happiest day of my life. My aunt Maria, who lived in United States, remembered her nephew in Colombia. I never threw away the box and I don't think I ever even played with him. I just looked at him and knew that everything was OK.

The True Hero

Today, I truly believe in what I am going to tell you. That action figure represented goodness, justice and the defense of the weakest before misfortune. He was a man who suffered in order to serve his country. A good man, who now used his life to serve others with his newly acquired gift of bionic strength. However, could someone help me in real life?

Years later, I began to have complications in my life, no-win situations. When sadness struck my adult life, Lee Majors couldn't put up with me anymore and the "Six Million Dollar Man" left the screen and fell into oblivion. Who could I rely on to help me bear this adversity?

When people talked to me about Him, I didn't think twice. I was told that He was born two thousand years ago, that He was the Son of God, that He promised life in abundance, peace, and rest to the afflicted. I didn't even think about it, I said yes, that I wanted to walk with Him… and from that moment in that's how it has been. Jesus of Nazareth came into my life with a simple invitation from me. He came, He healed and He continued healing my existence with every step. I found my purpose in life by serving Him and talking to others of His love and compassion. Peace, which is His stamp, is with me. So I don't have to wait six days to see Him in black and white.

****

Jesus of Nazareth came into my life with a simple invitation from me. He came, He healed and He continued healing my existence with every step.

****

Now, life is the color of hope. It is no longer framed in the sixteen inches of the black and white screen. Now, I can feel Him close to me, encouraging me to keep going, and saying, "Be not afraid, because I am with you, and be strong and courageous." As a result of this verses, I am stronger every day and I can even encourage those who falter and, in this way, He uses me in the life of others.

And you? Have you not received His gift yet? Well, prepare yourself, because sometimes parents pretend to have forgotten important dates, just to give us a beautiful surprise at the end of the day. Get ready and be happy, because your bionic man is wrapped up in a beautiful box and is just waiting for you to receive Him. Tell your Father in Heaven that you need His caress and be ready to receive it.

7

The Old Man with the Stick

H E NAME WAS Luis Ferro and I began to hear about this elderly man because people said he was a problem in our family. No one wanted to have him in their house and some of my uncles even had problems with their partners due to his long stays in their home. Although he was a nuisance now, years ago it was a different story and he had a prosperous life full of luxury and comforts. The lifestyle he lived before was completely different in comparison to the neglect he now suffered in the house of his daughter, the "divorcee," the diabetic, my mother.

What I Learned From My Grandfather

Perhaps my grandfather was a burden for all the family, but in my case he was an enigma who marked my life. After living in our house for quite some time, Mr. Luis Ferro was a complete stranger to me who never left his room. When he did, he never said a word. Our relationship was almost non-existent, until one morning when everything changed.

Before leaving the house my grandfather turned to me, and said something like, "Do you want to come with me?" I didn't hesitate and immediately accepted his invitation without even asking for my mother's permission. It was a marvelous, incredible day. What did we do? We started walking slowly, aimlessly I thought. However, then we arrived at a neighborhood park and he let me run freely. That was the beginning of the many adventures and lessons I would share with my grandfather.

I remember a special day when he lifted me up and let me hang from the monkey bars. He watched me and I stayed up there, clinging on with just my two hands and my feet hanging down below. Although it was maybe a meter's distance to the ground, it seemed like an abyss to me since I was so small at the time. He went to the other end and said that he'd wait for me there. I moved from bar to bar with difficulty and when I got to the other side, I was terrified and had cuts on my hands.

****

I showed him my hands and the blisters on them. He looked at them, looked me in the eyes and lovingly said, "They will heal, but now you will be stronger and tomorrow you'll cross those bars without fear".

****

He took a hold of me and put me on the ground. I showed him my hands there were now full of blisters. He looked at them then looked me in the eyes and lovingly said, "They will heal, but now you will be stronger and tomorrow you'll cross those bars without fear. Then, well... then you will teach your children too and you will remember me when I'm not with you anymore." We didn't say anything else. That day he held my hand as we walked home and I felt proud. At last, the wisest and strongest man I knew was holding my hand.

I don't know what emotional or physical difficulties you are going through at the moment. Maybe, deep down, you feel like a little child trapped on a high bar, with your feet hanging below and all you can see is an abyss. Maybe you feel like your hands are about to let go. You might even have fear in your heart. I don't know if this is a familiar feeling in your life. You might think that there's no one nearby to help, but believe me (and this is where I have authority to speak), that's how the feeling of defeat pushes into your mind. Maybe you have done something to try to resolve the situation, maybe your strength and sanity are at their limit, but this is the best time for you. When you have no strength left, you can open your spiritual eyes and you will see someone stronger encouraging you and giving you the extra boost you need to help you pass the test you are undergoing.

Holding God's Hand

In our culture, when a man becomes an adult, it is assumed that they should not have any fears or anxiety. It is also assumed that men do not cry or show any type of weakness. We are supposed to be like superheroes. Meanwhile, when women cry, you hear phrases like, "Are you crying again?" or "Please don't cr.y"

****

People don't want to see anyone suffering, but the only thing this achieves is to bury healthy feelings which should be expressed.

****

Symptoms of weakness are frowned upon. People don't want to see anyone suffering, but by hiding pain the only thing that is accomplished is burying all these healthy feelings that should be expressed. Over time, I began to realize that, as an adult, I felt a lot of fear and anxiety. The word "failure" made me tremble and being rejected by people brought stress upon me. I tormented myself thinking that I could end up as a frustrated man. Nonetheless, there was nothing more I could do in my defense. It was as if a rapid slide had taken control of my destiny and in a crazy race, I was turning into what I feared the most: a man full of anger and rage.

In many cases, fear can make us react disproportionately and can turn the smallest incident into a major problem. Then we lose control of our lives and the people around us feel hurt, whether that is what intended or not.

What can we do when the words of our loved ones are not enough? What can we do when good advice only helps us for a short period of time? What can we do when our good intentions fall by the wayside and we go back to our old ways? What can we do when grandpa's much loved and admired hands are nothing more than a memory?

It is time to give our hand to someone who can hold it. It is time to use resources that we have not used before. It is time to hold on tightly to our heavenly Father. I don't know your current situation but, believe me, the universe is just a prayer away. If you just hold out your hand in a simple act of faith, you will almost be able to feel the heavenly Father squeezing it and holding it.

****

Who is God in your life in this precise moment? He will be whatever you want Him to be.

****

It wasn't my grandfather's physical strength that made me feel safe. It was what he represented for me. Who is God in your life in this precise moment? He will be whatever you want Him to be. He will be your support, your teacher, your helper and your advisor, or just a vague religious concept in your existence. He can be the most important thing in your life or just another idea of something supernatural. He can walk with you daily and have a vital and real relationship with you, or He can become someone that people once talked to you about. Daily reading of the Word of God changed my concept of God as my heavenly

Father. Studying His word sustained me. Making His Word my own, helped make me a man with hope of change.

Just by praying to the Father at this moment, telling him to calm your fears and to help you in a specific aspect of your life, an invisible hand will reach out to show you that He is supporting you. Then, a feeling of peace and faith will flood your being.

It is time for you to rely on someone else rather than depending on your own strength. Feel free to express your fears to God. Jesus exposed His whole being to His Father and showed that He wasn't weak. He is and will continue to be the bravest man that has walked on planet Earth.

8

The New Boy's Life without Friends

I F YOU ASKED me how many friends from my childhood and adolescence I miss, you would realize that I lacked a social life. The truth is, I was never a very sociable person. My social circle was made up of my mother, my sister, a sick aunt, and my grandfather. My mother was an overprotective woman. I imagine that losing so many children at birth in combination with my father's abuse and a divorce fraught with threats, had put an end to the little emotional strength that my mother had left.

She saw enemies and danger everywhere. That's why I didn't have nightmares like other children of the bogey man or the monster in the wardrobe, instead mine were about my father. My most terrifying nightmares were about my father stealing me from my mother's side and condemning me to live with him again.

****

My most terrifying nightmares were about my father stealing me from my mother's side and condemning me to live with him again.

****

The emotional situation in our little family got so bad that I had hallucinations of my father in the street and ran away to hide from him, to later realize that they were fantasies that were a product of a terrifying fear of my father. His violence had the same influence on all of us. Even my aunt was a victim of my father's rage on more than one occasion. No one was safe, or at least that's what I thought at the time.

A Life with No Meaning

Who could save us? Nobody seemed to have the answer. Every time we arrived in a new neighborhood, we acted like a family in the witness protection program. We kept a low profile, we didn't socialize much and under no circumstances could I go outside alone. My social life was limited to playing with my sister and, when I could, watching the other kids playing on the street.

When I was registered in the neighborhood schools, I didn't go regularly, because everything depended on whether or not my mother's illness allowed her to take us to school that day. That's why I got used to being the new boy.

After a short time, when someone already knew my name and maybe even my surname, we had to run away from that place and find somewhere to move to straight away, because it seemed that my father had discovered our hiding place and that all his threats could come to life. When we got to our new location, the feeling of alienation came over me again and we stayed with what we knew: the television and the toys, which didn't really fulfill me anymore.

Around that time, I began to notice that I liked love songs. At night, when I couldn't sleep, I dreamed of another life where neither financial problems nor constant fear in our every morning were our daily bread.

A small radio with earphones allowed an FM station to fill my head with unknown words: spite, betrayal, disappointment, impossible love. They were all mysterious and attractive to me until the next day when I looked them up in my grandfather's old Larousse dictionary. Then I understood the songs and the following night, I understood more of what the singer wanted to express.

I started to believe that my mother was exaggerating the threat of my father. So, I rebelled against her keeping us locked up. "Why can I not have a normal life?" I shouted at her when I couldn't take it anymore, and she said, "Because you cannot," and that was the end of it.

****

Was that all there was in life? Fleeing from a crazy father and spending your life running away?

****

Indeed, was that all there was in life? Fleeing from a crazy father and spending your life running away? So, what about soccer? What about learning to kick a ball? Why can't I stop being the new boy? Why can't I be the one to laugh at someone for once and not be the one who runs away rushing to the security of his mother's apron?

There were no answers. At least, not at this point of my life; however, now I know the answers were there, even though I couldn't see them. The truth is that the majority of my traumas were solved when I went back in time to those houses and strange places that never really became homes. The answers were in those faces without a name due to our haste and our sudden escapes. They were also in the people who remained unchristen in my adolescent mind. People who I resented and maybe envied for years, but whose names I never knew, because the threatening ghost reappeared and we had to run away.

In the end, was the threat real or not? Was there really imminent danger? As an adult, I found out that my father had discovered where we lived again and that, once again we had to make our second escape, in a matter of seconds. From then onwards, although my father became more efficient in his search, my mother also developed great intuition and paranoia, which, on more than one occasion, literally saved our lives.

The Inevitable Result

However, something else was happening. Without realizing it, that instability was confusing me. I never knew if we were in the north or the south, if we were going through the city center or if, on the contrary, we were in the suburbs. At the end of the day, what was the point of paying any attention to the addresses if we never stayed anywhere very long?

With age, I kept the habit of moving often, not staying for much time in one place and having no close friends. I remember that, sometimes, I almost seemed to become someone's best friend, while deep down, I never let any relationship take root, be it love or a friendship. Why have a relationship when I would always, in some way, be the new boy?

Not being able to go out, to be with people my age, to know the streets or places where we lived, not only damaged my self-esteem and my image, but also turned me into a complex being who felt that regardless of what I was doing, people were looking at me and in some way laughing at me.

****

I didn't develop as a normal person. The inside me versus what I showed the world was completely different.

****

I didn't develop normally as a person. What was really inside me and what I showed externally were completely different. I became popular in some circles and, for some reason, girls went after me, but I couldn't give myself to them. I don't think I managed to be a good friend and, in some way, I always betrayed the friendship they offered me. And don't even mention love! Once I had conquered a girl, I got bored. Then, without anyone noticing, I went in search of the greener grass on the other side of the fence.

Life decided to show me that I was right: neither friendship nor love were for me. I was always the one who betrayed the friendship or fled from love; the one that couldn't remain peaceful for very long and got bored with a routine of everything being good and calm. That's the way I grew up, so what more could be expected of me?

9

Goodbye, Marina

ALTHOUGH MY MOTHER was a very young woman, she was very intelligent and she knew her life was slowly ebbing away. She knew that she would never see us graduating from high school and that soon, my sister and I would be unprotected. This young, beautiful woman was another victim of type 1 diabetes.

I remember that one day my mother seated my sister and me down and asked us what we wanted to be when we grew up. She gave us her reasons why we weren't obliged to go to any school or college and that if we had any talent or virtue, that she would help us develop it. She also told us that, if we had any dreams, no matter how insignificant or stupid they seemed, we should fight to achieve them. This was a huge proposition for me. I didn't know what my mother's true motivation was for saying something of such importance to us, although at the time it didn't really matter to me either.

****

> *I didn't know what my mother's true motivation was for saying something of such importance to us, although at the time it didn't really matter to me either.*

****

What would I know of her deepest fears and worries? I always believed that my mother was the most gentle, tender, innocent, and marvelous being on Earth. Knowing that she would die soon, she decided to only leave good memories for my sister and me. She wanted "her two little treasures" (as she called us) to remember her as the best mom in the world...and for me she was!

A Heavy Burden to Carry

If you have read the previous chapters, you will know that my childhood and adolescence were not very normal. On one hand, there was total isolation, the uncertainty, the almost complete ban on any social activity and on the other hand, the freedom to not study and do nothing. While other parents with children my age were pressuring them to get good grades at school or college, my sister and I, at eleven years old, were being given the choice to study or not. My mother was offering us the panacea, what almost every young person wants: the choice of not studying if we didn't want to.

Although this was a proposal full of possibilities, it was also a great responsibility for us, since we could not blame anyone else for our choices in the future. Beyond the argument of whether or not we were fit to decide at that time, far from all the moral and ethical implications, my sister and I were free to choose if we wanted to suffer the long, cold mornings in Bogota, the pressure of teachers and low grades and the fight to be accepted in the small societies represented by schools and classrooms.

****

How exhausting and despairing it is to want everyone to like you and to be popular! How stressful and panicking!

****

How exhausting and despairing it is to want everyone to like you and to be popular! How stressful and panicking! The pressure from teachers, classmates, grades and parents can cause such anguish that some people cannot even bear it.

While fleeing from my father, we ended up living in a neighborhood west of Colombia's capital. It was a working class neighborhood. Whenever my mother went grocery shopping or anywhere she thought it was dangerous for us, she would leave us with a neighbor. She was a teenager, but for us she was a very nice grown-up. She was possibly, the only person who could visit our house freely and play with us.

I remember that she was a very pretty girl, maybe even attractive. For me, that wasn't really important at the moment. Confinement and isolation meant that my male instincts developed slowly and normally. I didn't have the advanced hormonal development I saw in other boys my age. At that time, my conversations were pure and innocent. So, in this atmosphere, Marina, the girl who looked after us, was the best entertainment that my sister and I had ever experienced.

Marina's happiness and smile were contagious and she distracted us from everyday life and boredom, filling our time with her games and jokes. She played with us in a way that nobody would ever do again. I remember her arriving sometimes wearing her school uniform. At the time, she seemed very adult to me, very big, but she was only a little girl who was starting to grow up. She was probably fifteen or sixteen, but we loved seeing her sing or playing hide and seek, and believe me we didn't stop looking until we found her. As a matter of fact, we loved Marina.

A Difficult Resignation

One day, Marina stopped coming. We asked about her but no one paid attention to us. Marina never appeared! It was like she had never existed and that only my sister and I knew about her. We asked about her and everyone avoided answering us. No one wanted to discuss the matter. In the end, my mother talked to us. She told us that Marina had gone for good and that she would never be back.

I remember that I was sadder than I'd ever been in my life. My sister and I were overwhelmed. Marina had left us too. Once again, my heart had to accept the loss of someone I loved. So, for no reason, with no preparation, no goodbyes, just the emptiness, that lovely person was no longer in our lives.

****

> *So, for no reason, with no preparation, no goodbyes, just the emptiness, that lovely person was no longer in our lives.*

****

A few days later, my mother told my sister that Marina couldn't handle the pressure, because she was not a good student and she failed the school year. This meant that she couldn't graduate with her high school friends and this shattered her. Fear of her moody father and her mother's punishments had brought her to a dead-end. With nowhere to go and no one to support her, Marina took what she saw as the easiest way out. Marina took her own life, to avoid facing her parents' fury for failing the school year.

The truth is I didn't really understand what suicide meant. I only knew that Marina wouldn't be with us anymore and that was very difficult to accept. For me it felt like a betrayal, because she didn't want to be with me anymore. She no longer wanted to bring happiness to our lives.

With age, I realized that it was the opposite. My sister and I cheered up her life and distracted her. In fact, the time she spent with us was her best. She was distracted from the daily torture of her existence under the roof of angry parents who were obsessed with studying and who could not see the anguish in their beautiful daughter's eyes.

She needed them so much! But they could never realize this because they were not in their right mindset. They punished and hit her when she got bad grades. Now I remember the bruises and bumps on her legs. They were all a result of rage, the anger of parents who could never appreciate her.

Later, we moved from that area. We left behind Marina and her games, the hide and seek and her songs, her laughter and tenderness, her childlike happiness and her parents, who asked why she had done this to them when they were so "good" to her.

****

We left behind Marina and her games, hide and seek and songs, her laughter and tenderness, her childlike happiness.

****

A New Reality

Today, as years the years have passed by, I see that God allows people to touch and affect our lives in some way. Marina meant a lot to me, with her much needed happiness and amusement. I don't want to say it literally, but she was like a little angel who filled our empty existence with life, a caress from God in the middle of our despair. I could see His love and protection through people who, for a brief time, came into our lives. Moreover, He showed me that I shouldn't flee; on the contrary, I should bravely face adversity and never give up.

God talked to me a lot during Marina's short existence. Then, years later, life became very difficult for me in moments when disappearing forever would have been the easiest option. Times when I couldn't bear my own anguish and ghosts anymore. Circumstances when oblivion was more bearable than everything I had to face. I am referring to debts, illnesses, the death of someone I loved, the betrayal of a loved one, the humiliation of defeat, bankruptcy, and traumas that I hadn't overcome, or simply not knowing why I was here. All of this can make a person want to flee, to escape in any way and at any cost from an overwhelming reality which seems much too great to carry on the shoulders of men as weak as us.

That was how God spoke to me and affected my life in such an unforgettable way that I could never even contemplate the thought of running away. Marina made her decision and chose her path, but her life even in death continued speaking to me. I couldn't follow her path and leave behind so many unanswered questions. I couldn't leave such an important question for those who loved me. Personally, I couldn't follow Marina's footsteps. Heaven had yielded my path preparing me to follow other footsteps: in the sandals of a Carpenter and Fisher of men. We will always have two paths to take, two sidewalks to follow, one leading to life and the other…. well, I don't think anyone is interested in the other.

****

I understood that fleeing wasn't for me, that I should passionately face everything that intrigued me and terrified me.

****

I understood that fleeing wasn't for me, that I should passionately face everything that intrigued me and terrified me. At the beginning it wasn't a clear reflection, it wasn't something that I determined at a certain time. It was a vague idea that, with the years, started to grow inside me. I had the option to follow the example of Marina or that of my mother, who clung onto life trying to help her children and pleading to heaven for another day of existence.

MARIO FERRO

In regards to my mother's initial question, my sister and I decided that we were artists, that we both enjoyed the arts and that we would dedicate our lives to singing and acting. My mother brought us together again and gave us everything she could at the time. It was like her living inheritance. She gave us enough to enroll in a theater school, a school that would become the starting point for a life full of excitement.

My sister and I could not say goodbye to Marina and we never spoke about her again. Her name was never mentioned in our house until now. How did I remember her name? Maybe I kept it in my memory for this moment. Maybe it was too painful to remember. Maybe we had the same questions as her parents. Maybe we will never know, so...*goodbye dear Marina!*

10

The White Wall

WE LIVED IN a very big city. I know this for certain because we used to constantly move to different neighborhoods; that is why I can actually say we knew the entire city. This time, the change was radical, like everything in our lives. We were at the opposite side of the city, it was a dramatic move. We immediately moved to a small rented house, which was suitable for the tight budget my mom managed so well.

What My Grandfather Taught Me

My grandfather Luis easily adapted to the new circumstances. Once again he took me out to know our neighborhood. His hand didn't seem so big anymore but he thought he could still guide me on this new path that our family was on, and we went towards a forest full of pine trees that seemed to reach the sky. The smell of the forest was strong and it permeated our clothes in such a way that it was as if we had bathed in pine.

Grandpa told me that people got together there in the mornings to go running and get fit. So, if I wanted, I could start running to become more agile, faster, and healthier. He also told me that if I was observant, I would learn things that I would never forget. He said, "Look at the details, learn to observe while you are running. It seems like a contradiction, but with time, you will understand."

*I ran a lot among those trees, as if I was trying to
escape from someone, as if by running, I could leave
behind so many things that I didn't understand.*

I ran a lot through those trees, as if I was trying to escape from someone, as if by running, I could leave behind so many things that I didn't understand. I ran quickly through the pine trees, barely avoiding them. During my race, I kicked through the fallen leaves and dry pine needles that were stopping the grass from growing around the trees. Endless and confusing paths were formed... paths that didn't lead anywhere, that didn't lead to any escape route. In that forest, I learned that the faster I was and the more I wanted to escape from those ghosts we call memories and painful thoughts. As I became more skilled and agile, those feelings would just overwhelm me even more.

My grandfather told me that our memories don't catch up with us, we catch up with them. At the beginning, we leave them behind for a while. Then, with the twists and turns of life, we find them again. It is like fighting with someone who will always be waiting for us in the same place and that every time we pass by, we will have to look at them face to face. Painful memories, hate and regrets are not left behind, they are learned, assimilated and passed to our children and to those we love.

They are the inevitable inheritance that no one wants, but we all receive and those memories show up without an invitation. It is like an embarrassing illness, that no-one admits to having, but that everyone has. The hate, ancestral fights, insecurities, flaws, and madness present in every family are genetic illnesses that no one wants. However, they stay with us until the day we die. That is what my grandfather used to say.

Unfortunately he didn't know any other path and that is why he followed this one until the end.

****

The hate, ancestral fights, insecurities, flaws, and madness present in every family are genetic illnesses that no one wants. However, they stay us until the day die.

****

An Unexpected Surprise

One day that I was given some running shoes as a gift. I went to the forest and set off without stopping, pausing or looking back, following the winding paths created at random at the whim of this huge forest. I thought that its abundance would never end. It was like everlasting life, like an existence of perpetual adventures. I felt slightly afraid, since I had never gone so far by myself.

That day I went out without my sister. I ran and ran until I had no energy left. I don't know how many hours I was running for, but at last, and to my complete disappointment, that immense forest suddenly ended in front of me, with no warning, no signs. An enormous white wall loomed behind the last tree. I couldn't believe it. I had reached the end of the path. Everything ended there; there was nothing else to see, just a wall, a white wall, strangely built there… and then the end.

****

With age, we realize that life, just like that path, is hard and sometimes we wish it would end.

****

During my *entire* past life, I thought our existence was like that forest. When you start *a new path* full of energy and with **new things**, just like *my new pair* shoes, the arrogance of age lets you think *that journey* will never end. *As time passes*, we realize that life, just like that *journey* is hard and sometimes we wish it *would come to an* end. *In spite of those feelings*, we *manage to regain* our strength, continue our lives *but*, with no warning, the white wall suddenly *gets in the way* and death takes over each of the memories, the complaints, and the hardships. That's what I thought then.

The New Effigy of Solitude

I remember that on a typical cold and wet day in Bogota, I felt a chilly atmosphere of never-ending nostalgia. On one of those *endless* days, my grandfather slipped *on* the street *while* leaving home and banged his head. He was immediately attended, but there was little that could be done. *That* beautiful, old man left my life as quickly as he had come into it, leaving an indelible mark of wisdom and love in my life, different to anything I had ever experienced. One day in April, the white wall reached Don Luis, or he reached it. It doesn't really matter. He went down one of those paths and never returned.

The image *ingrained* in my memory terrified me. I learned to fear death in an incredible way. The way my dear grandfather's life ended scared me and that's why I avoided going to his room, which remained locked. Apart from being afraid, I now had to face my solitude. My grandfather was my only friend in a neighborhood where kids didn't play in the streets out of fear of being knocked over by the cars which were quickly leaving the city.

****

Apart from being afraid, I now had to face my solitude. My grandfather was my only friend.

****

My solitude grew, and for the first time I felt the emptiness that my mother talked about so much. *So this was life*, I thought, *going from here to there, suffering, losing friends and loved ones on the way.* Where was my friend? My buddy? My confidant? Where did he go, leaving me in *this* boredom?

The days *passed* as if a huge black cloud was above that house. Nothing took my mind off it. I only thought about him, and why he had left me. Every day, I asked, *"Where did you go grandpa?"*

God *responded*

My mother was very sick. She had gone into a diabetic coma and was in *the* hospital. My poor sister could not answer any of my questions. I thought to myself, "So this is life… walking and walking, getting tired and finally, a wall, and then nothing". My mother couldn't die then. We were still too little to be without her. I needed more time before the diagnosis of my mother's illness was fulfilled along with all the nightmares that tormented me. I wasn't prepared to live without her or to lose her.

This was the first time that I became cynical, and began to fill my thoughts with silent arguments against the faith and God that my mother insisted in telling me about. I looked for the book that she respected, the Bible, and with a cry of anguish I opened it and found the phrase: "If you have faith as small as a mustard seed, you can say to this mountain, 'Move from here to there,' and it will move. Nothing will be impossible for you." (Matthew 17:20). That was the message I needed. I talked to God and said to him: "I have faith, help me! You can't take my mom now, we need her. We're not ready to face life without her. I know you can do the miracle!"

*I talked to God and said to him, "I have faith, help
me! You can't take my mom now, we need her.
We're not ready to face life without her. I know
you can do the miracle!"*

There was no lightning, *nor* flickering lights. The Bible
didn't move. There wasn't even a small gust of wind in the
room. Instead, something incredible happened. The next day,
my mom was discharged and recovered miraculously. The God
who I had fought with that day had listened to me, had come
through for me. Five years later, when my mother died, I was
ready to take care of both myself and my sister.

Meeting Nelly

Years later, after studying and working hard, I was already
involved in *modeling* and became a professional model. I was
contracted to appear in a soap opera which needed many
models. I was told that day the actress who I had wanted to
meet for a long time, would be there. When I arrived at the
location, she was already there shooting a scene. *As I stared at
her*, I said to my friend with complete certainty, "Someday, I'll
go out with that woman." My friend laughed at me. That day
we didn't even exchange a look or a word. I don't think she even
saw me, but I was sure that it wouldn't be the last time that our
paths would crossed.

*By chance, I was called to take part in a soap opera
whose leading actress was this very same woman*

that I had decided years earlier would go out with me, Nelly Moreno.

****

Six years later, when I was already a theatre and television actor, *by chance*, I was called to take part in a soap opera *whose* leading actress was *this very same* woman that I had decided years earlier would go out with me, Nelly Moreno. Well, now the possibility didn't seem so ridiculous. *In this* soap opera, I was going to play the role of her husband, so we would be sharing many scenes together. The meeting was exciting, *I would like to think*, for both of us. Maybe, for her, it was "love at first sight"... I don't know, at least that's what I say!

How would I have imagined that this woman would be the one to introduce me to Jesus, the savior of my life? It was obvious that she was already a Christian. All her behavior showed me fervor, security, and faith in a love that I desperately needed to find. God used her to get my attention, to make me see the possibility of a real, loving, and true God. Thanks to her testimony, I began to open the door of my heart to the possibility that would lead me to making the most important decision in my life.

That soap opera with its lead actress came into my life during a difficult time. After many more losses, cynicism had completely taken over and the only thing I really wanted was to die. Once I had achieved so many material things I still felt just as empty, my mind drifted to thoughts of why human beings were on Earth if there was nothing more than suffering. This meant that nothing would make you happier than resting in a grave. However, there, in my place of work, was my way out, right in the place where we were shooting the soap opera.

The White Wall is Not the End

Then Nelly invited me to her church. It was the first time that I went to a Christian church and it all seemed dreamlike to me. That night I gave my whole life to Jesus Christ. Three years later, in that same church, Nelly became the leading actress of my life's soap opera. Before God, we promised to love, accompany, and support each other until the end of our lives.

That day I understood that the white wall was not the end of the journey. There was something else behind the wall, and someone else had overcome it. Someone who, two thousand years ago, showed us that *the life of a man* did not end with death and that death was just the prelude. Someone *who* showed us there was *so* much more. Someone who jumped over the white wall, took off his shroud, crossed to the other side, and came back to tell us about everything there was behind it. Someone named Jesus showed us that the pine trees led the way to all types of lush, beautiful vegetation, that the waterfalls and rivers framed a never-ending destiny by his side. He who walked in the valley of death and came back victorious, told us that man's journey led to death, to those paths full of ghosts, hate, and painful memories. Jesus walked in the valley of death and returned victorious in the same way that we will do in every difficult moment of our lives if we decide to walk with Him. What is indisputable is that He knows the way, He is the way.

****

God still indulges me and tells me that if I make sure that He is the most important thing in my life and in my heart, the replies will arrive, because they are already on the way.

****

The forest is no longer there, nor is the wall. I would never be able to have discovered what was in that place. So, twenty-six years later, God still indulges me and tells me that if I make sure that He is the most important thing in my life and in my heart, the replies will arrive, because they are already on the way. I would have loved *for* my beautiful grandfather to know what was behind that big white wall! I would have loved *for* him to know that life doesn't end there, that the journey continues after physical death, and that we choose the path to take after that moment!

If you still haven't done it and you want to receive this *gift* that will change your life, it is very easy, since it is just a prayer away.

> *If you confess with your mouth the Lord Jesus and believe in your heart that God has raised Him from the dead, you will be saved. For with the heart one believes unto righteousness, and with the mouth confession is made unto salvation*
>
> Romans 10:9-10

11

The Extent of Success

A S A RESULT of the hardships I faced throughout my childhood and adolescence I was determined *to* never be poor. I decided that, by all means possible, I had to be rich and admired in this world. On many occasions, I saw how my mother had to disguise us, literally, to hide all signs of our precarious economic situation. The money our father gave us was barely enough to live on, and it was difficult to *make it* to the end of the month. Our closest family gave us what they could, and some of them were very generous, which is something that I am still grateful for to this day.

I remember they used to bring us products from the market, which they generously shared with us. I also remember we were invited to a children's piñata party at a relative's house. Our visit to that beautiful house, where there were children, clowns, food, and fun, was something very special for someone of my young age who didn't normally go to places with so many people.

****

Our visit to that beautiful house, where there were children, clowns, food and fun, was something very special for someone of my young age.

****

That day seemed like paradise to me, but we didn't even last ten minutes there. The child's mother, told my mother that we should not have gone in that attire. Apparently, our clothes were not appropriate. So, before we suffered any further humiliation, my mother got my sister and me out of there.

I remember that I couldn't stop crying on the bus ride on our way home, but that was the way things were with my mother. There was always a lack of explanations. The truth was that she wanted to blame herself, and that we wouldn't understand the reality of what had happened. While in my father's house we lived a life of comfort and luxury, away from him we were just *mere* disadvantaged children.

My father made us understand his message perfectly, "With him everything, without him nothing." That's how we lived, between the charity of more fortunate relatives and my mother's careful and masterfully implemented measures. Phrases like, "There is none," "There's not enough," "We can't," and "Not today, another day," became part of our daily life. So, my anger and rage started building due to us always being needy, the "poor ones" of the family.

Obsessed with Money

When I was an adolescent, I was desperate to make money. That's when I decided to get into the world of show business. At last, it wasn't only acting and music classes. Now, I wanted to earn money doing what my mother had allowed us to study for years.

I got into the world of modeling, and soon I began to appear in television advertisements and fashion shows all around the country. From modeling, I went on to theater and then onto television. I soon made a name for myself and became relatively famous and well-known. The internal anger I had pushed me to achieve things that others couldn't.

****

I felt powerful, invincible and began fighting with anyone that even looked at me.

****

Every day, I ran through the streets, I played basketball and football and went to the gym regularly. I felt powerful, invincible and began fighting with anyone that even looked at me. I appealed to that rage and the being that was inside me to "help" me at those times when I needed to become a beast.

That's how I destroyed faces with my fists and didn't realize it until the fight was over. Then, when I reacted, I had to flee, to get out of there. I couldn't bear my own conscience or look at the damage I had inflicted. According to my twisted judgement, anyone who dared to mess with me got what they deserved.

What Was Inside Me

Arrogance took a hold of me and I became a "leader" among my friends. I gave advice on how to get women and recognition. I saw people as objects and friends as steps to put my feet on in order to advance. Women meant nothing to me. However, if I could use them to my advantage in any way, I also stepped on them to advance in life.

I was handsome and on television, I was considered to be a gentleman or the lead actor of soap operas. So, all my complexes of inferiority, poverty, deprivation, humiliation, and abuse, hid behind the face of the gentlemen of the moment.

I was walking on clouds but the reality was that no one who really knew me could have loved me. The truth is that I was not loyal, I was not a good friend, and I was not good in any way. I only helped myself and my own interests. I don't even remember my first girlfriend or my first kiss, since it must have happened in between stepping on someone and humiliating someone else.

****

I don't even remember my first girlfriend or my first kiss, since it must have happened in between stepping on someone and humiliating someone else.

****

At that time, I had not accepted Jesus into my heart. I was so busy trying to forget the pain in which our father had submerged us that I was unable to think about anyone other than myself. At times, I felt like I belonged to a heavenly world, I believed I was an Adonis, a demigod and that in some way, I was transmitting this to those closest to me. However, I was unable to escape the reality inside me which was hidden by rage and struggled to remain unseen. The fear of failure never disappeared; it only remained hidden for a certain period of time.

One day, we were shooting at a hotel and I remember we had been working until late the night before. We were shooting outdoor scenes, so we were out of the city. I was exhausted and an assistant decided to be the "funny guy" and bang on my door to call me to makeup. My nervous system was very fragile so anything could rile me. He gave me a terrible shock and I got to the door quickly, opened it and asked what had happened. The man replied rudely and didn't even apologize. He said something to me and in that instant, I transformed. I threw two chairs against the wall and the man ran away. I ran after him, barefoot and in my underpants. The man ran to the street immediately.

Although the entire soap opera crew was there, I couldn't stop myself as the assistant ran around the entire parking lot. I wanted to hit him and never stop. Some men threw themselves onto me and I could hardly control myself. I vaguely remember what happened, these details were told to me by my friends who were witnesses to this whole situation.

I didn't care about my work or my reputation. My internal "friend" gradually acquired new arms of destruction with no need to hit. I learned to say words in an intelligent, evil way that destroyed people inside and hurt them without leaving any apparent trace. I learned to be scathing, cutting, and ironic. When I couldn't hit or hurt with my fists, I did it with words. Over the years, my arsenal grew exponentially. The violence inside of me expressed itself through fists, kicks, breaking doors, throwing objects, cursing, being rude, and offending the feelings of others.

****

My career took off, meteorically, and my internal "friend" grew just as fast.

****

My career took off, meteorically, and my internal "friend" grew just as fast. Yes, according to this world's standards, I was successful. But, where was God in my life? In the arms of the men who threw themselves on me and didn't allow me to destroy that careless young man who annoyed someone he shouldn't have during the shooting of a soap opera.

I cannot count how many times God saved me, how many times he protected me and surrounded me with His angels, even if I didn't notice.

12

The Stairs to the Second Floor

THE HOUSE WHERE I was born and raised had three stories. The strange thing is that the house where my three children were born and raised had the same number of stories. In the seventies in Bogota, it was very common for the stairs to have tubular, brightly-colored handrails that went from the floor to the ceiling. The stairs were made of granite with very sharp edges and right-angles.

The imprints of violence

One day, my father, my mother, and I were on the second floor of our house. At the time, I was about six years old and he was having a heated discussion with my mother. Suddenly, he transformed into the beast that was always reappearing in our lives. His face changed and a monster took control of him. How could someone so clever and intelligent transform into a beast in a matter of seconds?

Maybe, only those who have lived or suffered such an experience know what I am talking about, although in many cases, people forget in order to move forward.

****

Maybe, only those who have lived or suffered such an experience know what I am talking about, although in many cases, people forget in order to move forward.

****

The argument continued in the Ferro house. However, it was just from my father's side, because my mother was retreating towards the stairs that led to the first floor. He was harassing her and pushing her, while I tried not to see or hear. Even when I covered my ears, I could still hear her screams perfectly. My mother wasn't talking anymore, because the beast before her had taken control and had even hit her. I realized that the stairs were very close, while I heard more shouts, more rage, and more fury. It was as if they had given him an excuse and the demon had been set free, or maybe not, maybe he only came out when he wanted to. I don't know. I don't remember.

What I do remember is my fear, the terror, the impotence, and the feeling of injustice. I admired him. He was my hero, my father. However, the person in front of me was no longer my father, it was another person. Someone who only spat out curse words and enjoyed using terror to control everyone in the house. Another blow and the stairs were closer and my mother had her back to them. I only thought, "Mom, turn around, look, stop," but I couldn't speak, I was mute, paralyzed. Six years old and I already knew him, I had seen the devil in person and I lived in his house, in hell itself.

****

The cold, hard granite stairs crushed the fragile body of a woman as beautiful as my mother.

****

Another blow and another step backwards. My father hit her again and she fell down the stairs... The cold, hard granite stairs crushed the fragile body of a beautiful woman. I didn't cry, I didn't shout, I was just a silent witness of her pain. I don't know what else happened. He was shouting things like, it was her fault for provoking him. How can anyone look for blows to the face and to be thrown down the stairs? Then, he calmed down. The madness left him. The anger that had possessed him subsided in order for him to be overcome by guilt.

At some time the strength of that dreadful anger leaves you so that you become the victim of your own conscience, so that when you wake up and see what you have done, your soul is destroyed and it's easier to continue than to undo what is already done. He saw her lying there, beaten and he left her. He left murmuring to himself and mumbling about his own impotence to fix what he had done. When she appeared in front of me again, she was crying and walking slowly. I was hidden under a table where the telephone was…a table that was barely big enough to hide me.

It was made of very thin black metal and thin colored cork strips. The truth is, that table didn't hide me from anything, but I thought it did, that there, in some way, I would be safe from the devil, from the demon of rage and fury that possessed my father. But, how could I be safe if I lived in hell? She passed by me on her way to the bathroom. She was going to clean her injuries, but just as the table didn't cover me, the water didn't repair the humiliation and terror that was inside each of us who lived in the house.

****

I swore that no one would abuse me in that way. I don't know why, but instead of swearing to protect my mother, I swore that no one would ever abuse me. I would stand up to any injustice in my life.

****

I swore that no one would abuse me in that way. I don't know why, but instead of swearing to protect my mother, I swore that no one would ever abuse me. I would stand up to any injustice in my life and that I would defend myself from anyone who tried to knock me down. Without realizing it, I hated my mother's role as the victim. I didn't want to be like her, beaten and humiliated by a powerful and inflexible being. So, without even thinking about it, without even noticing, I invited that demon into myself. I allowed it to give me the strength to defend myself, to be like my father and not like her, the victim. It's crazy! Isn't it? However, that's the human mind. Many people choose the feeling of self-protection which brings them to the same point as me, violence, different forms of violence, but in the end it's still violence.

History Repeating Itself

Many years later, when I was already married with children, my son had started walking. For me, that was all a father could want for his baby. I was already a full-grown adult and I loved playing with him and running around our three-story home. I never had the temperament of a controlled, normal person. Every now and then, I had attacks of anger, which included scenes of rage and shouting. If anyone bothered me, I attacked them in whatever way came to my mind at the time. I never "allowed" anyone to abuse me. In the few schools that I attended, I stayed for such a short time frame that I don't remember much about them. However, if anyone bothered me, I hit them. A supernatural force invaded and possessed my whole being. I loved it... I really enjoyed it. I never lost a fight in the streets and I had a lot of them.

One day while playing in my house, my son did something that really annoyed me. It wasn't anything in particular but, in my world, anything could annoy me and make me mad. So, I gave him a push, and my son hit his nose on a step. Suddenly, I saw blood on his little face and it was as if my conscience came back... my useless conscience that made me shout like a mad person until my wife came out of the bedroom and saw me with the child in my arms.

She literally wrapped him up with her body and took him off me. She immediately realized what had happened and walked away saying things that reached my conscience. I can't describe the pain I felt. There I was, on a different staircase but, just like my father, hitting and injuring someone I should be protecting. I was alone, trapped by a despair which I had never experienced before, although it was perhaps the same despair that my father had felt when he threw my mother down the stairs from the second floor.

****

Where was God when I did that? There... right there, giving me the chance to see in my conscience what I was doing and letting me decide my own and my family's future.

****

Where was God when I did that? There... right there, giving me the chance to see in my conscience what I was doing and letting me decide my own future and my family's future. His love allows me to write these lines and, if you accompany me, you will discover how God's love arrived and changed everything in an extraordinary way. On several occasions, I have talked about this event, but not in such detail as I am in this book. I have even told it in front of my son, who remembers absolutely nothing. But, I remember it very well. I will never forget it, I can't and I must not, because it is my insurance not to go back to that staircase.

The Love of the Father?

Shortly after I converted to Christ, the preachers at church were talking about an inexplicable love, a love that was difficult for human beings to understand. In those days, when I was told about God's love, I couldn't accept all of it. The truth is, I could never understand it. They talked about having a relationship with God. They said that God loved me and that in heaven there is a superior Being that loves his children. A Being that protects them and cares for them. He listens to prayers, no matter how small they may seem. I was also told that there was a Book inspired by His Spirit and that I should read it to hear His message of love.

Although I didn't understand all of this at the beginning, it seemed like a good idea and I decided to try it. I saw people on this new path who were happy and joyful. All of them told stories of how their lives had changed when they found this great and marvelous love. For me, it was like beginning to live the way others wanted. I forced myself to believe in that truth that was so beautiful and sublime, but when I arrived in my room to pray, I didn't feel anything. I often felt ridiculous, as if my words were bouncing off the ceiling. In the end, I got bored talking to myself and I ended up falling asleep or turning on the television.

****

Over time, I turned me into a cynic, into an unbeliever who wrapped himself up in the blankets of faith and the church.

****

Over time, I turned into a cynic, into an unbeliever who wrapped himself up in the blankets of faith and the church. Ultimately, I was an atheist in the middle of a group of believers, who didn't want to admit his doubts in case of being rejected from this new community. A community in which, for the first time in his life, he felt that he could stay and belong.

I thought that I had avoided everyone's gaze and scrutiny, but my wife was watching me closely. Eventually, one day, she said, among many other things, that I could not escape God's immense love for me. She told me to look deep within myself to find the reason that I could not receive God's love or accept His forgiveness. I insinuated that she was confused and that her message was probably for someone else, not me. I tried to convince her by my actions that I was very spiritual. I told her that I had already forgiven and even preached the gospel and that many people went to church because of me.

With stubbornness, the woman told me that no one could deceive God, and that I was running away from Him. She told me to stop fleeing from my Father's love. When she said the phrase to "stop fleeing from my Father's love," it was like if she had opened Pandora's Box. I said to her, almost losing it, "What Father's love? Do you want me to tell you about a father's love?"

I shouted at her, asking how I could believe in a father's love if I had spent my whole life watching my mother suffer at the hands of my earthly father. I confessed to her that the bitterest memories of my life were due to the emotional damage inflicted on me by a man who took out all his anger on his children and his sick and defenseless wife. I told her that, if anything, I was in this state because of a father who never knew how to take care of his children, who never wanted to listen to me and who, when I most needed him, wasn't there for me.

****

How could anyone even insinuate to me that there was a good father? At last, everything I believed came to the surface.

****

How could anyone even insinuate to me that there was a good Father? At last, everything I believed in came to the surface. Something came out of me that I never imagined I had inside. I had a deep hatred and resentment towards the male figure as the head of a home. I had an unhealthy anger for the role of the man of the family. I grew up believing that men were the parasites in a marriage. I thought males were deadbeats who were only useful for reproduction and afterwards should simply disappear. As for the mother, she just had to raise the children. So I despised the role of father as much as possible.

A Messenger of God

Was this belief true? Did I really believe those thoughts were true, or were they just my way of hiding so that I didn't miss the protection, care and love of my dad? God used this woman to uncover that part of my life. She helped me understand myself. That was how I understood that the scared child was still inside me, crying out for a father that loved him while, at the same time, not wanting to be hurt or let down again.

This woman told me that, if I wasn't prepared to face that experience, no matter how hard it was, I would never be healed, much less be able to help others who were suffering as much, or more, than me because of the wounds of a tormented and frustrating past that wouldn't go away. She even said that I would never achieve this if true forgiveness did not take place in my shaken and damaged soul.

Then I asked her what I should do. She explained to me that, above all, I had to understand that my heavenly Father was not like my father on Earth. So, I had to accept how damaged I was and receive my heavenly Father's love. She told me that forgiveness was vital at this stage. However, I insisted that there was no bitterness within me.

****

So, I had to accept how damaged I was and receive my heavenly Father's love. She told me that forgiveness was vital at this stage.

****

This was another extremely hard stage in my life, because I thought I was a very good person who was suffering. So, how could I ask for forgiveness for my sins if in my mind I was like Mother Teresa of Calcutta and Don Quixote de la Mancha? The fact that I had helped my sister, aunts, and uncles economically for years, confused me. In the end, I gave up and told her how I felt inside, what had been accumulating within me for years.

I never saw my father as a protector. On the contrary, I saw him as someone who wanted to destroy me, he was a distant and dangerous person who didn't accept me as I was and for whom everything I did was tantamount to failure. I realized that the new being she was asking me to accept disturbed me. Unconsciously, I was associating God the Father with my earthly father, a father who deeply wounded me. I was prepared to escape from God, no matter the cost. Although I could accept religion, the Bible, the groups, and communion with people on the same path, I couldn't even get near God the Father without it hurting me. That was why my heart was closed, why I always fell asleep when I was praying, and why I couldn't even lift up my hands to surrender myself to Him. To tell the truth, I was accustomed to running away from my father.

I discovered I had spent my life fleeing from my dad, running away from one house to another, hiding from him, his bad temper, his rage, and his threats. However, the truth was that he was residing in me.

****

She put her arms around me, told me to close my eyes and started to talk to me softly.

****

She put her arms around me, told me to close my eyes and started to talk to me softly. She began by telling me to accept her embrace on behalf of God and that she was offering herself so that I could receive the embraces that I never received. It was also a way for me to receive all the tenderness and affection that I had no received from my dad.

Believe me, I was a hard man, but at that moment I gave in. I couldn't hold in my tears. It was like a hoarse voice coming from the depth of my soul and crying all the pain it had within. In some way, I was grieving the loss of a father that I wanted to love and that I never really got to know. When that woman let go of me, I didn't know how much time had passed. Her clothes were wet from my tears. I didn't know how burdensome they were since, at the time, I felt like I was floating. Miraculously, my pain was purged and I felt that, maybe now, I could accept the closeness of a God who I was being encouraged to call Father.

A New Love Story

Father? What a beautiful, deep, and respectable word! What was that? What was wrong with me? Well, I was starting a new love story, a story of the most sublime love that can exist. The love of a good Father for his child. Now I could walk with Him without fear, without fleeing. I could stay and listen to Him and say anything to Him without being afraid that my words would bounce off the ceiling. I could tell Him how much I loved Him and how grateful I was to be able to believe in Him and feel Him present in my life. By the way, the woman who did all of this for me, is my beautiful wife, a powerful healing instrument in my life.

In response to my previous question, I can say: the Father's love was always manifesting itself my life. What I mean is, changing something bad into something good. Why "good"? Because, as a result of all my experiences, today I can tell you my story and give you hope. If God could change me, he can change you. It is at times like these that it is worth bringing up the past. The Devil tried to destroy me and those I love, but Christ came to change everything and to give us a fulfilled life.

****

The Devil tried to destroy me and those I love, but Christ came to change everything and to give us a fulfilled life.

****

No matter how much I failed Him, God is the perfect Father and He will never fail me. If you have many sins, you will be forgiven. As a result you will love Him and your life will be a constant eulogy of praise that will lead you to serve Him. Helping others in such a way that your life will have a great purpose. What glorious hope!

13

The Other Grandfather

THE CHILD COULD barely breathe because he was undergoing something that nowadays would be considered a form of torture. He was six years old, lived in his home city, a place that is cold all year around and where the plants have the dark green hue of the earth because the climate "obliges" them to.

At that time, his dad was punishing him for losing some coins that he had given him to go and buy breakfast. It was almost sunrise, barely six in the morning, and he had been put in the stone water tank where the clothes were washed. His dad took him out and put him under the water again until he almost fainted. This action was repeated until his father's rage had subsided. His father believed that this form of punishment would help mold his son so that one day he would be a responsible and honorable man.

Then at the young age of six, the father threw him on the ground and left him naked in the yard in order to learn his lesson. His mother's shouts did not help the situation. She blamed him for being disobedient and for being a bad son by provoking his father's anger. She took him, still undressed, and slapped his cheeks and back leaving them with red marks.

The Past and its Repercussions

Shouting, insults, abuse, and humiliation were normal for this child who grew up harboring his anger and silently cursing. He was unable to defend himself and what he sees before him is too big for his young age. He promises himself that one day he will escape, that he will leave everything and go away. He swears to himself that he will be a better person than his own father, but he never managed to be different.

****

What happened? Why, if he wanted to be so different and he was brave enough to do it, did he not achieve it? Something tragic happens in the lives of human beings.

****

What happened? Why, if he wanted to be so different and he was brave enough to do it, did he not achieve it? Something tragic happens in the lives of human beings. While some people desperately try to distance themselves from the image, ways, and manners of their parents, others decide to be the complete opposite and live a tormented life trying to escape from the mold that formed them. In the second case, the others amazingly become their own parents and end up being identical or even worse than the original mold.

The first group, that is, those that don't want to be like their parents, try their hardest to be different. However, the more they try, the more latent the memory becomes and they suffer more torment, rejection, and internal pain. There is a pain in their soul because of the past. They wish they could travel in time in order to be different but they soon realize that this is impossible.

The second group gives up and accepts that things in the past were handled correctly and they disregard the fact they will destroy their existence. The reality is that there is no way to escape the past without defeating it first. The past cannot be buried, it needs to be resolved. The past is like matter itself, it doesn't disappear, it transforms. The past is only forgotten through physical illness and, even so, still prevails in cases of amnesia. The past mysteriously regenerates itself in the present and intervenes in the future of human beings. No matter how hard they try, no one can avoid it. No human can defeat it. The past is something so powerful, that people repeat it unconsciously.

How to Break with the Past

Without remembering the past, humanity would be lost. So, what can you do to be different? How can the human species improve and not be condemned to relive the mistakes of their parents and grandparents? How can we stop perpetuating the disaster of others and not leave this inheritance to future generations? How can I be different from my father, without hating him and without destroying his memory? How can I avoid condemning myself to be like him? The answer is easy: without the intervention of a miracle, of something from outside it is impossible.

This transformation element is not earthly, it comes from above. It is called forgiveness through understanding, compassion, acceptance, and goodness. Human beings can turn their past into the most valuable thing in their life. The past can have a force to transform that is more powerful than the biggest hurricane on Earth or the strongest earthquake that has shaken our planet. Two thousand years ago, a Jew left us the formula and it is within the reach of those who need it and want it.

The Meetings with My Father

That child who was a victim of physical and emotional abuse was my father. His dad was "educating" him the only way he knew, the way he had been taught by his father before him. When we examine this situation, we can see that this way of "educating" children has passed from generation to generation, without anyone daring to contradict it or stop it saying "Enough! Let's stop evil, violence, anger, and humiliation in human education."

Now, I am convinced that there is no real way of escaping without divine intervention. My father learned to educate and teach children in a misguided manner. So, he never contemplated the option of being different from his own father, or maybe he did, but he ended up repeating the family tradition with me, his own son.

****

My father learned to educate and teach children in a misguided manner. So, he never contemplated the option of being different from his own father.

****

Even with all the fear my father instilled in her, my mother had to sue him before the civil courts. That's how she obtained money to raise her children, because her unstable health prevented her from working, meaning that she did not have many options. The lawsuit made my father even angrier. However, after several threats, he decided to obey the law, in his own way. Every month when he gave my mother her check, he insulted her and cursed every cent he gave us. With time, the anger became frustration and finally, resignation. In this way, my mother had a way to get by.

I remember that one day my father did not deposit the monthly installment to my mother's bank account. Because of her illness, she could not go pick up the money from him. So, for the first time since the divorce, I had to meet my father. I was only about nine years old and I will confess that I was terrified. I still remember going into his silent, dark house (my father suffered from terrible migraines, so the windows were always closed and the light never entered where he lived).

My eyes had barely adapted to the darkness when I heard his voice coming from his bedroom. He uttered two curse words, pointed at an envelope on a table, told me to take it, and to close the door behind me.

That day, I didn't see him, I just heard his instructions. I followed them as quickly as possible and ran out of there as if a ghost was chasing me. I left that house with my heart beating rapidly, but that experience left me with a tremendous feeling of emptiness. What must my father's face have been like? Why was he so annoyed with me? Those questions were left unanswered for quite some time until, my mother explained to me that I would have to go to my father's work to pick up the money from him every month.

This time, I arrived at a huge building where I was given instructions to find a specific office and who to ask for once I arrived. I followed the instructions to the letter. A little later, I was told to wait in a corridor and I stayed there for a few minutes. Then my father came out and at last I saw him. He looked strong and tall, but his face was barely hiding the fury he felt seeing me there, reminding him that he was obliged by law to give us that money which he wanted to keep for himself.

****

Again, he handed me an envelope and started to swear about my mother, me, all of us. He took me to an emergency stairwell and started shouting at me, getting angrier and angrier.

****

Again, he handed me an envelope and started to swear about my mother, me, all of us. He took me to an emergency stairwell and started shouting at me, getting angrier and angrier. As soon as there were no witnesses, his face changed immediately and he started insulting and making derogatory comments about my mother. I was just listening and it seemed incredible to me how quickly he was speaking. I thought that he would hit me. So, I took the envelope and began to run down the stairs, without looking back. It was as if a monster was chasing me, as if my father, who had changed into a beast, could reach me. I don't remember how I got home, just that I would never forget that day.

Fear was building up again in my being and my soul. I never wanted to be like my father. I never wanted to see him again, but throughout my adolescence I saw him numerous times. My father never managed to be different from his father, in the same way as his father couldn't be different from his father before him. This curse, this "spirit," this demon, passes from generation to generation and incredibly perpetuates itself within families. It survives time, overcomes geographical barriers, pollutes entire surnames and God only knows how long it has been walking on earth without anyone standing up to it and daring to wipe it out of their life.

The Key That Opens Doors

Where was God when I was suffering my father's abuse? The truth is that it was his plan for me in life, to be able to be able to continue breathing so that I might turn into something different. Remember that only a miracle can change our past and that that miracle depends on heaven. Even the most painful memories can be enough fuel to positively change future generations in order to be better people despite the past.

Today, I think about that child, abused on the cold mornings, that child who, one day, would become my father. Today, I understand him, in the midst of his pain, his childhood anguish, his wish to escape to somewhere else. I got to know this child through the few stories that my mother told me about him and about why he became violent.

One day, my paternal grandfather saw one of my mom's sisters in the street. He hated her because he thought that she had helped my mother escape from his son. So, he shouted at her, insulted her, and hit her, in broad daylight in front of witnesses. Even though he was already an elderly man, his anger was there, unabated, proud, and indifferent. He never changed. His skin was worn, but inside he was still intact. I made the decision that I would not be like my grandfather. I decided to break that inheritance. Although, every day, those memories seemed more distant, they were still there like a subtle shadow, efficiently interfering with my present.

****

Forgiveness is the key that opens the door to every jail.

****

That day, thanks to the mercy of God, I could understand why my father was the way he was, and knew that I had to forgive him. However, I needed help from heaven, because I wanted it to be real forgiveness. So, I asked God for help and I prayed. When I did I experienced one of the most beautiful moments of my life. Forgiveness is the key that opens the door to every jail. Bitterness was keeping the trauma in my life alive. What great freedom! This revelation from God was a beautiful present!

If you want to feel this freedom, say a prayer of forgiveness now for all those who have hurt you, especially those who affected your childhood. Those people do not need your forgiveness, they might never know you have forgiven them. Maybe they're no longer alive. However, it is you that needs it. Say a simple prayer, asking God to give you strength to make this decision and do it. Feel real freedom and find the true love of a Father that doesn't fail you, that loves you as you are, will never leave you, and will always give you everything you and your family needs.

14

"Mario, Why Are You Like This?"

SINCE I WAS a child, my anger made me shout, break things, curse, knock people over, and hurt people with my words. I would especially hurt those living in my house... my family. It's ironic, but we always hurt our loved ones first and they are also the ones we hurt most. Unfortunately, when you have this type of behavior, anything makes you angry and it doesn't matter if it is a major incident or an insignificant detail.

****

Unfortunately, when you have this type of behavior, anything makes you angry and it doesn't matter if it is a major incident or an insignificant detail.

****

Any event is enough motive to explode. Whether it is an internal frustration, the impossibility to communicate, a rumor, libel, a misunderstanding, a moment of tension, a difference of opinion, an unfulfilled wish, or something out of your control. In a nutshell, many things can cause anger in a human being and result in an unavoidable emotional explosion, which frees their anger and rage. I am sure that many people can identify with these symptoms that end in an uncontrolled explosion.

Why change?

According to the descriptions my wife, Nelly, has given me during an episode of ranged I would transform and my face completely changed. The color of my skin, my eyes, and my voice all changed during the explosion of anger. During this explosion I wanted to offend people, I had a wish to break or throw things, I cursed, and practically destroyed any special moment.

Shortly after the explosion I would curse at myself for my reaction. It is like a volcano that goes out to give way to a cycle of justification for the explosion. You feel the need to justify your actions and then a quick transition to feeling bad follows. Then, you look for someone other than yourself to blame for so much anger. Next, comes denial, saying that you didn't shout that loudly, that things didn't happen that way and you invent another scenario, freeing yourself from any responsibility.

****

Next, comes denial, saying that you didn't shout that loudly, that things didn't happen that way and you invent another scenario.

****

In many cases, the person doesn't really remember what they did or said. On many occasions, losing control in that way, led me to this type of situation which, of course, I denied. I would like to highlight this amnesia, the act of not remembering very well what you do or say, which is true to some degree.

I particularly remember a day in 1996, when we had been married for some years and my children were still small. I had just done another one of my "shows." I can't really think of any other way to describe it as a result of my professional career as an actor which is ironic. At the time, I shouted, threw something against the wall, slammed a few doors and said a few curse words. In a nut shell, I transformed into that monster that came out in my house every day.

On that occasion, while I was going up the stairs, my wife said to me from the second floor, "Mario, why are you like this? Why can't you change?" She said it gently, pleading, as if she was begging me to listen to her. As if by a miracle of God, I listened to her. That day I heard her but, above all, I listened to my own reply. I said to her, "Why do you want me to change? So that everyone walks all over me?" But, what did I really want to say to her? Sometime later, I began to understand the meaning behind my response.

The Help That Comes From Above

Before, I told you about a time when I was a child, that my father hit my mother. In my innocent mind I believed hiding under a very small table would be enough to shield me from my father's rage, from the monster living within him. However, the truth is that, by hiding, I was making a decision. I understood that there were two types of people: victims and aggressors. In other words, aggressors treat people badly while victims allow other to treat them badly.

I didn't like my mother's role in this scene. Unconsciously, I decided to be like my father. I don't know if others decided differently, but in my own experience, I did not become a protector. What's ironic is that I became a photocopy of my father. His bad example did not help me make the decision to be the opposite of him. Instead, I decided that no one would treat me badly and that's when all my problems began.

If you read Ephesians 4:26-27 (NVI®) in the Bible, the apostle, Paul, gives us the key to what happened in my life that day:

"In your anger do not sin:" Do not let the sun go down while you are still angry, and do not give the devil a foothold."

In other words, if you get angry, don't allow this to make you sin. Also, *you should not let your anger last all day, because if your anger lasts, the devil can take advantage of the situation.* The next questions is: What happens when the anger lasts for your whole life, camouflaging itself, hiding in the depths of your soul, and lasting forever?

Up to that point of my life, I had been living like this for more than twenty years. There were a number of factors that blended together to form the perfect jail, a prison that had one sole prisoner, me. My jail consisted of many bars such as the bad example of my father, the man who I ended up imitating as the result of my decisions based on my fear of being a victim.

****

I decided to try to get "good" results from this behavior in some way, since I felt extra strength for day-to-day life.

****

I decided to try to get "good" results from this behavior. I felt as if I had extra strength for my day-to-day life from having that attitude and conforming to being that way. Moreover, due to the lack of external help, I was scared of change, of being unprotected, of not knowing how "to be" any other way, of the ignorance of not understanding that I was mistaken. In fact, all these factors, and many more, end up making change very difficult and almost impossible for any human being.

That was when I needed divine intervention, the spiritual part of life that is not very well understood in this world. I had to abandon my ego and my fear and allow God to come into my life. In those moments, we need to call out to heaven for help. I must emphasize that my beloved wife never stopped praying for me and for my complete conversion to Christ. She never confronted me with arrogance and never used the arms of this world to tackle what resided within me. She never viewed me as her enemy, because she knew that something else was acting inside me. The wife that God gave me never stopped blessing my existence and secretly interceded with Him for my change and liberation.

****

The Bible teaches the importance of having a place to talk with God alone and that we should confess our anxieties to heaven.

****

The Bible teaches the importance of having a place to talk with God alone and that we should confess our anxieties to heaven. Why? Because there are beings that us humans cannot defeat by ourselves. So, when you feel like you can't go on, we need to resort to another type of fulfillment. We need to replenish ourselves with another type of energy. We need to get our breath back in order to achieve triumph in one final and powerful effort.

If you feel that your strength or the strength of some you love is at its limit, maybe it's time to look for that quiet place, that room, that secluded park, that peaceful lake, or to just close your eyes and ask for help from above, so that God can show you the way. This is the first step to obtaining the key to freedom, and in my case I was about to obtain that freedom something that would change it forever.

15

Taking Stock of the Damage

I CAN'T REMEMBER how many beautiful moments I destroyed in my times of madness, how many of my own and my dear family's birthdays, how many traumatic experiences I imposed on those who I love most, after God, nor how I negatively affected those around me. Words can barely express the years that were wasted on trouble and problems, fighting and shouting, as well as misunderstandings.

I remember that one day, Nelly surprised me for my birthday. She had set up an office with new furniture and a new computer, as well as a party-serenade with mariachis included and lots of guests and food. I remember that when everyone had left

I was really annoyed. I didn't know how much money it had all cost. It seemed like a waste of money to me. So I complained to her until she started crying.

****

Every walk, every memorable event, was marked by an argument and, of course, the pretext was always something insignificant.

****

That wasn't the only time. I also did this during some of my children's birthdays as well as some of hers. Even went we went out to eat, I caused a lot of scenes in fancy restaurants or wherever we were, making Nelly quickly leave. Every walk, every memorable event, was marked by an argument and of course the pretext was always something insignificant.

What Lies Behind Everything

Living with a tormented person is very hard to do and I can see that today. How can we not see the spiritual side of this situation? If I want to be a certain way and I can't, I know that how I am acting is wrong, but I can't avoid it and I don't fight it, I am defenseless against something stronger that lives within me. As a pastor, I know that sin is in the flesh, in human beings, but I am referring to something much bigger, much stronger, and I can only find the explanation in the Word of God itself.

The Bible says that we have a great struggle against things that are in the atmosphere and that we don't see. That our battle isn't against people. In Ephesians 6:12, the Bible tells us that the struggle we have is against spirits who want to impose their authority in today's world:

> *12 For our struggle is not against flesh and blood, but against the rulers, against the authorities, against the powers of this dark world and against the spiritual forces of evil in the heavenly realms.*

So, we should look beyond: *What lies behind people?* And instead ask ourselves: *What is inside them?* The Scripture also teaches us about unclean spirits and spiritual entities that torment humans:

> *14 Now the Spirit of the Lord had departed from Saul, and an evil[a] spirit from the Lord tormented him.*
>
> 1 Samuel 16:14

28 When he arrived at the other side in the region of the Gadarenes, [a] two demon-possessed men coming from the tombs met him. They were so violent that no one could pass that way.

Matthew 8:28

A Sad Existence

Today, I cannot describe my own situation in any other way. That's how I felt, tormented, without peace and without happiness. I understood what Jesus of Nazareth did for me on the cross. In every Christian meeting, I said to myself that Jesus was the Lord. Every Sunday, I went to Christian services and worship, I sung a few hymns and I got tremendously bored. I tried to pray, but my mind always told me that I seemed ridiculous. When the Christians prayed and we held hands, I often saw how everyone bowed their head and closed their eyes with fervor and passion, saying prayers that seemed endless to me. Meanwhile, I was a mere spectator. I observed them without getting involved, liberating the struggle which was constantly occurring deep within me. I lived in this way, in silence and fearing that the other believers would say I was evil, because they seemed so full of the Spirit, so saintly and so in control.

Going to church was my favorite time for an argument, driving aggressively, and scaring my family. If my wife was taking too long to get ready, I would start complaining. If she "made me" go somewhere I didn't want to go, I got mad. If she made me visit her family, she would pay for it later in the night. I would make her pay by completely spoiling her evening. If she forgot something in the house and we were already in the car, I berated her for the whole journey and was annoyed for the rest of the day. Buying clothes, travelling, going for walks, eating, visiting people, and getting to know people... all these things that are positive for people, gave me the opportunity to become bitter and to spoil things for others.

16

Where Does My Help Come From?

I CAN'T DENY that despite the bitterness that lived within me, my family was able to experience some beautiful moments. I have always loved my wife and my three children. I would give my life for them and would have done so in those days as well. So, the issue was never a lack of love, but the impossibility of giving this love in an appropriate, healthy and creative way, my difficulty to be happy. That was my precarious situation.

Getting up from your last fall, living defeated by that "other me," feeling ashamed every day because of the previous day's outburst, the anxiety of asking for forgiveness for something and not knowing if you will do it again... these things torment you. However, I looked for freedom in a church. I had confessed my sins since childhood, I even confessed to things that I hadn't done. I fasted, prayed, regularly went to Christian services, and read books. I also helped cast out demons, sang hymns, raised my hands to heaven, and asked for pastoral advice. I watched Christian television and listened to Christian radio, I went to healing services, I received healing hands, prophecies were declared over me, and I even got christened. Despite all my efforts I was never free. I continued living with that torment of acting as a believer in front of others but as a crazy, hysterical person in my own house.

Another Part of the Process

In 1996, we decided to go to Miami, Florida to attend the conference of a very well-known preacher, who prayed for the ill and those oppressed by demons. I went hoping to find more of God in my life, but it was terrible, I couldn't feel anything, no one could help me. My beautiful wife faithfully accompanied me everywhere and became an expert in these matters and a prayer warrior.

****

My beautiful wife faithfully accompanied me everywhere and became an expert in these matters and a prayer warrior.

****

I have to emphasize that I do not want to give the impression that my wife was some kind of masochist who liked sharing her life with a professional torturer. No, she is a woman with a very strong character. Maybe that's why she had the internal strength to put up with me and help me, because she always stood up to what was inside me.

She often came up to me when I was about to cross the line with my kids, and without caring about the size and weight difference between us, she would put her face in front of mine and, looking straight into my eyes, she would confront what she said was inside me. She was speaking to a demon, which, according to her, was living inside me or was taking control of my life.

They were very strange and uncomfortable situations, but the incredible thing is that I reacted, dropped the matter, and left the room where she was. When Nelly spoke to the entity within me, I felt slightly crazy and couldn't resist it. I picked on her or I just reacted with a nervous laugh and pretended to forget about the matter. If no person could help me, what would? In Psalm 121, the Bible tells us that our help comes from heaven, from the heavenly Father:

> *I lift up my eyes to the mountains; where does my*
> *help come from? My help comes from the LORD,*
> *the Maker of heaven and earth.*
>
> Psalm 121:1-2, NIV®

And, in some way, that's how it happened... What I am going to tell you next comes from a materialistic, humanist, skeptical, practical and, at times, even incredulous man. It is something that happened to me and to which I bore witness.

17

The Man in My Bedroom Door

ONE DAY, MY wife came running to me excitedly telling me what she had discovered in the Word of God and that although she had read it many times before, it was now a revelation to her. She was convinced and wouldn't stop until I listened to her.

Nelly said to me, "You aren't like the Gerasene demoniac described in the Bible [Matthew 8:28-34], you are conscience of it, you keep it there by your own will, you are the owner of your house [your body]". She was referring to my whole being, my body, my mind, my soul (Matthew 12:29: "You have the control and you are in charge, but in some way you are in alliance with that demon. You must bind him and throw him out, and be sure to keep him at a distance [Matthew 12:34], because no-one else can do it for you. We have already done everything humanly and spiritually possible".

****

"You have the control and you are in charge, but in some way you are in alliance with that demon. You must bind him and throw him out, and be sure to keep him at a distance".

****

I should point out that, in my adolescence, due to my parents' divorce, following my mother's family's advice, I visited a psychiatrist and a psychologist and I underwent many physical and psychological examinations, x-rays, scanners, and every type of medication available. I passed all the questionnaires without a problem. My intelligence quotient was a little higher than average and they never found any signs of bipolar disorder, brain irregularities, or epilepsy. I have never had hallucinations nor taken drugs. I have exercised all my life and now take part in highly competitive sports. Thank God, my brain is completely healthy.

So, what was bad within me? Why could I not be happy? Could my wife be right? Perhaps a demon or an unclean spirit was tormenting me and I didn't realize it? Was it permanently living within me? Did it just possess me at times? Was it beside me constantly influencing me?

The Challenge of Freedom

One afternoon, Nelly exhorted me strongly. It was very respectful but at the same time firm. We were still in Miami. The three children, who were still small, were resting in improvised beds that we had set up beside ours. She said that I should seriously consider the possibility of what she had been talking to me about. Her theory was that, when I got angry, I wasn't myself and it wasn't just simple anger. I was, literally, another person, that she called the green man (referring to the Hulk, the comic book character who was a normal person that turned into a monster when he got angry).

I laughed and picked on her for a while, but she insisted. She gently cornered me. So I made some jokes about the possibility of a demon being behind my life. However, this time I couldn't escape. There was something in her pleading look that made me understand that God was using her in my life that day, like many others. At last, I was ready, so I listened and asked her sincerely, "What do you want me to do? I don't think it's like that. My condition isn't so serious. I don't feel damned or possessed. I only react when you all behave badly."

****

"What do you want me to do? I don't think it's like that. My condition isn't so serious. I don't feel damned or possessed. I only react when you all behave badly."

****

She continued to insist and was determined not to let me out of that corner. Her beautiful eyes shone with authority and love. Her quiet, soft, romantic voice was begging me to listen, even if it was just once. She basically had me with my back against the wall. I asked her again, "According to you, what should I do?" With a smile, she said, "Throw him out. Get the strong man out of your house." I laughed again and she explained to me that if I wasn't convinced, I wouldn't throw him out with conviction and that the demon would return every time I needed him.

Suddenly, her face lit up, because she remembered a well-established dynamic that we had when one of us wanted the other to do something. She said, "Let's bet that this time God wants you to be free and that you must see what is inside you. If you ask him sincerely to show you the garbage that is tormenting you and hurting us all, God will show it to you. Do you want to bet that you can see it?"

Knowing my competitive spirit, she had given me the perfect formula to accept so the only thing left to do was to start the challenge. Nelly gave me precise instructions that started with me on my knees, saying the prayer that she had prepared for me to repeat after her. It went like this:

Holy Lord and Father: I ask you that, if there is an evil influence in my life, please let me see it and be free from its torment. I ask you this in the name of Jesus of Nazareth. Amen.

I got up from the ground and with a slightly jeering smile I hugged her for her dedication and care. I saw her as a whimsical little girl and me as the big brother who kept her happy by saying that yes, Superman did exist. Being completely honest, at the moment I didn't feel anything, I just wanted the problem to be over and for her to leave me alone. Then we had dinner, watched some television, prayed, and went to bed.

A Terrible, Liberating Experience

When I opened my eyes, it was early morning and it was still dark outside. Nelly was lying by my side, in a deep and peaceful sleep. On the other hand, I felt anxious and scared. Suddenly, the door of the bedroom started to slowly open. A figure, that was taller than the door itself, emerged. A dark, sinister figure, whose face I couldn't distinguish, but who was an enormous man. He was very well dressed, completely in black, a black that was darker than night itself. I started to feel very scared. I wanted to speak, but I couldn't. I tried to shout, but no words came out of my mouth, not even a sound, anything that could catch the attention of my wife or children.

****

The figure gradually came towards me and I tried to get out of the bed, but I was completely paralyzed. Then, my fear became panic, because I was watching it advance slowly, steadily, fearless before my anguish.

****

The figure gradually came towards me and I tried to get out of the bed, but I was completely paralyzed. Then, my fear became panic, because I was watching it advance slowly, steadily, fearless before my anguish. Suddenly, it bent down and literally, sat on top of me. My panic became terror and I began to feel things I had never felt before. Then, the man in black put his huge hands around my neck and started to strangle me, and I couldn't do anything. That man was ending my life in the presence of my wife and three children and I was completely immobilized.

I started feeling suffocated and I couldn't breathe. My thoughts mixed together and I couldn't do anything until, at that precise moment, a light brightened in my brain and I immediately knew that this had to do with the bet had I made with my wife that afternoon. The short prayer I said a few hours ago was the reason I was now in this terrible situation. I regretted everything, my skepticism, my harshness my stubbornness. Now I knew what was happening. I could see it with my own eyes. I could feel his hands tightening around my throat and the weight of his body on mine. I could also feel his fury, his rage, his hatred, and his wish for death and destruction. I met him face to face that night, but maybe it was too late.

****

I could feel his hands tightening around my throat and the weight of his body on mine. I could also feel his fury, his rage, his hatred and his wish for death and destruction. I met him face to face that night, but maybe it was too late.

****

I clearly remember what I thought: *My God, forgive me, I did not know what I was saying, I regret everything, my skepticism, the hardness of my heart, my contempt for my wife and the pastors...*

and soon, his name came to my mind: *Jesus, help me, Jesus. Jesus, save me. Jesus, come to my rescue.* In my mind, I told that presence to leave in the name of Jesus and then as if he had no choice, as if I had spoiled his plan to finish me once and for all, he started to let go of my neck. So, in my mind, I kept repeating Jesus' name as much as I could and I told the unclean being to leave in the name of Jesus. Immediately, he stood up. He looked enormous and blocked the little light coming through the door, which was now completely open.

I had always laughed about ghosts. I played jokes on my cousins and aunts about ghosts. Also, I was always happy and proud of myself for being a strong, brave man who didn't believe in that sort of thing. However, there I was, lying like a rag, at the mercy of this enormous figure that was now lowering his head to leave the room the same way as he had entered it. In that moment, he looked at me one last time and then he left.

****

As soon as he had disappeared, I got my voice and movement back. I was trembling and I began to cry internally without any tears.

****

As soon as he had disappeared, I got my voice and movement back. I was trembling and I began to cry internally without any tears. I took my wife by the hand, called her name and woke her, shaking in terror. My eyes said everything. She woke up and, without having to explain anything to her, she saw me shaking and anxious. Straight away, without me having told her anything about my experience, she said, "You saw him, didn't you?"

She gently took my hand and led me out of the room. She hugged me and we stayed like that for a few minutes. Only then could I cry. Thoughts were running through my head and I was trying to find out if what had happened was only a nightmare. While I was thinking, my wife was letting me process everything with affection, as if she had always known that this moment would arrive, as if she had always been committed to me, my life and our ministry.

18

A Simple, Powerful Prayer

AFTER THE EXPERIENCE I talked about in the previous chapter, I was able to relax at last. Then, Nelly came up to me and said, "Well, now that you have seen him, it's time for you to get rid of him, for you to reject his protection, that little bit of extra strength that he always gave you. You have to be weak again, so that you can trust the new strength that God will give you. Now, your strength will not come from a demon, but from God's love. Your whole life and being will change today, forever."

First step: Recognition

Before her words, I remembered that day when my father hit my mother in front of me. I relived the moment when I decided that I would never be the victim. In a way, I had just made a pact with the devil, letting that spiritual power that had lived for generations in my father's family, enter into me.

Kneeling before God, holding my wife's hand, I fervently and passionately followed her prayer word for word, convinced that I would be free. In the name of Jesus, I got rid of the power within me and I ordered it to never enter or act in my life again. That morning, was a humbling experience. I understood that in the spiritual world there are many things that human beings do not understand.

****

*When I finished praying, I smiled. My wife's eyes
shined more than ever, because God had used her
immensely in my life.*

****

When I finished praying, I smiled. My wife's eyes shined more than ever, because God had used her immensely in my life. She wrapped her small body, which now seemed enormous to me, around me...in that moment Nelly, was and still is, a giant for me in terms of anything to do with God. We melted into a spiritual embrace that has lasted until this day, since we are still embraced and united in God.

The sun was setting and the light of the beach was starting to come through the window. It was a new spiritual day and the light was filling not only the small apartment, but my whole being. The light of Christ was starting to manifest itself within me.

With time, I have seen how the victims of abuse swap their roles throughout their lives. Sometimes, they become avengers, people who can't stand "injustices" or attacks against the weak. At other times, they are unable to see that they are the unfair ones, the ones who walk over others and hurt them. In my case, my role was always clear to me, I was always the aggressor.

Second step: Freedom

The road to freedom was not easy, but even afterwards, I had to struggle each day to keep that peace, that freedom from hell. Ultimately, that peace must be maintained and fought for at all times. Enemies exist, especially the enemy of God, who is always sniffing around to see when it can catch you off guard.

Little by little, I made steps towards change. However, it took me a few years to discover the new Mario or, more specifically, the original who was hiding behind a veil of hate, pride, anxiety, traumas, complexes, doubts, insecurities, arrogance, and scorn.

No one believed that the change happened overnight. Although I understood that the demon had left, my flesh was contaminated, used to being one way and not knowing how to be any other way. I had to get to know myself. At last, I saw that I could live in peace, that I could be a loving person, that I could give words of affirmation without fearing that someone would obscure me. I learned to see the value of each person, how different we all are, how marvelous every life that God lets me touch is. I accepted that every human being is marvelous and beautiful in the eyes of God.

Today, people surprise me, I appreciate them and like them. People are my passion, in such a way that I do not fear interacting with them. I cherish them and can listen to them because I really want to get to know them. Despite this, I cannot say that I didn't fall or go backwards.

I can still remember the first time after my encounter with that horrible figure that I got annoyed and shouted. I felt terrible because I thought that nothing had changed. However, with time, I understood that these reactions were occurring less frequently. I realized that this was a process, something like a strong earthquake and its aftershocks. After a strong telluric movement, these aftershocks come in a systematic way, but they are only the result of a major movement. So, you know that they will stop at some point.

****

Now I had to walk on this path to freedom holding the hand of Jesus Christ.

****

That was my case... my flesh was tainted, but I was a free man. Now I had to walk on this path to freedom holding the hand of Jesus Christ. Since that unforgettable day in 1997 when I saw the being behind my torment, things have changed a lot. Gradually, I changed from a beast into a person who was the complete opposite. The change wasn't only in terms of anger. With the anger, came the control, the bitterness, the hate, the revenge, the resentment, the hardness of heart, the complete lack of compassion, the judgement, the pessimism, and the deep discomfort that others' happiness caused in me.

It was difficult to be around me, because the arrogance, pride, and that false sense of security never allowed me to give in. I was never wrong, the guilty party was always someone else. My capability for hurting people was immense. With only a few words I could lead someone to depression. I had so much stress that it was affecting my health. I had a stomach sickness for over ten years, I was unable to process normal food and at times even water would be painful to digest. I lost a considerable amount of weight and at one moment thought that this sickness would kill me.

However, glory to God! He was able to bring a permanent change to my life. I know that with my own strength, I could never have been truly free. Even today, men that knew me in my past are shocked by the change. They say I am a new man and, for some time, it was difficult for them to get used to the new Mario.

Today, I am careful with my actions and to not hurt those around me. I made many mistakes in the past and I still do. Although I know that I am nowhere near perfect, there is no denying that God freed me.

Third step: Restitution

After the spiritual liberation comes the "decontamination," getting used to the new me. A very important and painful step is restitution. It is important to be aware that this is a very difficult, but necessary, step. The loved ones who were hurt should be given the chance to forgive. You should approach these people to tell them that you are deeply sorry and show your regret, with the strong resolve of not doing it again. This will, undoubtedly, free the offended person as well as the victim who was under Satan's oppression.

It is important to be aware that, perhaps, some people are no longer in our lives or do not want to forgive us. However, we should not see this as an obstacle to continuing our life of freedom. It is also true that there are people full of bitterness or with scars so deep that they want to leave us stagnated and stay with their vision of us in the past. We should not allow any of this to bring blame to our lives, because we need to be better and free in order to serve the Kingdom of God. It is about being free to serve, to be useful, to have peace, and to be a testimony to others.

The path to follow is shown to us in the Gospel of Luke when Zacchaeus repents, finds the truth, and understands the scale of his sin. As a result, he wants immediate restitution:

> *Then Zacchaeus stood and said to the Lord, "Look, Lord, I give half of my goods to the poor; and if I have taken anything from anyone by false accusation, I restore fourfold.*
>
> Luke 19:8

In my case, I spoke clearly with my wife and I showed her that I understood what she had lived with and put up with by my side. I did the same with my children and those who worked with my in the ministry. I asked for their forgiveness and radically changed how I was with them. Through the guidance of God I have been able to show them the way and tried my best to compensate their love, patience, and understanding towards me.

****

It is important not to do things emotionally, not to be led by the carnal impulses of the conscience and to let God's Spirit guide us every step of the way.

****

It is important not to do things emotionally, not to be led by the carnal impulses of the conscience, and to let God's Spirit guide us every step of the way. This is not a game. It is a very serious matter, involving lives and people's future and should not be taken lightly. What works in one case may not work in another. So, we need to be guided by suitable, professional, wise, and loving people.

Prayers and fasting are very good resources for discovering and listening to the word of God. Sometimes confessing things and speaking about forgotten issues with the wrong people, can only make the situation worse. Along with the change there comes blessing one way or another. The freedom you have in your life will also bring freedom and peace to your loved ones. If restitution is not available at this time, start your new path with no blame on your part.

19

Pulling Down Strongholds

THE UNCLEAN SPIRITS, the demons, the entities of evil, operate in many ways. They do it through thoughts, through possessing people, and through their evil influence, creating an unhealthy atmosphere around them. All of this can combine in ways that we can't even imagine, but their objective is to kill, steal, and destroy.

For example, if I started chatting to someone and they began talking nicely about another person, recommending them in some way, I would take this as a personal insult against me. I would find some way to say something negative about that person. If someone else was praised, applauded, or admired, it made me feel tremendous dissatisfaction and made the emptiness inside me even greater.

****

*If someone else was praised, applauded, or admired,
it made me feel tremendous dissatisfaction and
made the emptiness inside me even greater.*

****

I don't know if people noticed, but my wife did. She would confront me and this would lead to another argument. I spoke badly of people that weren't present and enjoyed finding out what others said about me. In this way I filled up my "fuel tank" of hate and revenge. I told other people's secrets and created dissent. I thought I was the only one who deserved praise and when I didn't receive it as much as I would have liked (*I wanted to be constantly exalted*), I attacked those who did.

I wanted to have faithful friends, but I couldn't be one. In every romantic relationship I had, I felt dissatisfied and I passed that feeling to every woman who had the misfortune of accompanying me at some moment my life. I made every girlfriend feel that no one was enough for me. Dissatisfaction is a prominent characteristic of these types of malignant influences, in order to keep the mind and soul tormented, something in which they take great pleasure.

Why am I telling this story?

When I realized that few people talk of these matters, I never wanted to confess my errors in public. Many believers are taught to avoid these issues, while others are ashamed to even admit that they are being tormented by evil spiritual entities.

I should point out something very important: I do not want to start a doctrinal debate since there are believers who have a specific belief on these matters and I don't want to offend them. Neither do I want to take a particular theological stance. I just want to tell my own personal experience, which, as such, is just as respectable as anyone else's. It is my life and that's why I am telling it how it is.

****

The only thing that matters is to let the truth be known, and the truth in each of our lives is Christ, to know him, but also to be free to serve him better.

****

As a preacher, a pastor, maybe I should be more worried about appearances and be more politically correct. However, I can't remain silent, because image doesn't matter, it doesn't matter what people will say. The only thing that matters is to let the truth be known, and the truth in each of our lives is Christ, to know him, but also to be free to serve him better.

For many years I could not serve him since I used my time to be angry, fighting over nonsense. I spent half my life causing pain and dismay to others and the other half asking for forgiveness and feeling bad. So there wasn't a lot I could do to positively contribute to the lives of those I loved. It is important that many people going through this experience know that there is a way out, a solution. That is why I am telling my story, why I am giving my testimony today.

Clarification

I would like to stress that the lives of Nelly and my children were never in danger because of me. I never hit my wife or physically abused her. The aim of this book is not to tell any person, be it a woman or a man, a girl or a boy, to live with a potentially aggressive, harmful person. Our intention is to clarify that, even in cases of extreme violence, a person can be free if they really want it.

A person can distance themselves from the aggressor, preserve their life and, at the same time continue to pray and intercede for their life. Our weapons are not from this world, they are spiritual and destroy the power of evil in our existence:

> *For the weapons of our warfare are not carnal but*
> *mighty in God for pulling down strongholds.*
> 2 Corinthians 10:4

Born to Serve

NELLY DANCED SINCE she was four years old and became part of the Colombian National Ballet. Then, when she was older, she moved on to television and national cinema. My wife became the most well-known dramatic actress in our country in her time, earning huge amounts of money for her talent, loved by television, and adored by young people.

My career shone, but never as much as Nelly's, since I retired early to follow and serve the Lord. I gave up everything at the peak of my acting career. Those who know me, know that's how it was. When I met Christ, I fell madly in love, but he also brought clarity to my mind. The truth is that I wanted to have a family, a home, to grow old together with my wife and to have the respect of my children and grandchildren. I knew very well that my acting career would make this goal difficult to achieve. So, I changed my priorities.

****

> *I knew very well that my acting career would make this goal difficult to achieve. So, I changed my priorities.*

****

We have always had a healthy economic life. We have travelled all around the world together. We have enjoyed all types of comforts and stayed in luxurious hotels, but we have also lived in very modest homes. We have sailed in yachts and enjoyed everything that comes with a life with money. For short periods, we have also experienced shortages and restraints. Throughout all of these times, I must say that my wife always honored her vows to be with me in both richness and poverty. She never complained in those difficult times. On the contrary, she helped me find new ideas to prosper and never stopped believing in me as her husband and the father of her children.

We created the first Christian television program in our country. We had a nationally aired program telling real-life testimonies of what God can do in a person's life. We wrote and produced a musical comedy containing a message of faith and love in God. This comedy was shown in the main theaters both in our country and in others, leading many people to give their lives to Christ.

****

My wife became a member of Colombia's National Congress, preaching in public meetings to senators, representatives, and even Presidents of the Republic.

****

We have organized acting workshops and we have had radio programs in the United States praising God. My wife became a member of Colombia's National Congress, preaching in public meetings to senators, representatives, and even Presidents of the Republic. We have preached the Gospel everywhere that God's love has taken us. We have founded various churches, which to this day, are working to bring the message of salvation, one of them is located in Bogota, Colombia.

We are currently working in our church in Miami, Florida. This local church is growing day by day with the love of God and it is full of young people who love God with all their might. Our ministry works on a daily basis to try to conquer whole cities for Christ, so that families reconcile and parents and children come together in a project for a greater life.

Our three children serve in the ministry for the glory of God and we spend every day making disciples from all across the world. Due to our origins and professions, the arts and media are very important in our ministry. We love to write and produce our own shows. Therefore, at the end of every year, more than one hundred young people take part in all types of musical performances so that thousands of people can learn about the love of God.

****

We have ambitious plans with God, to make sure His Word reaches the ends of Earth.

****

We have ambitious plans with God, to make sure His Word reaches the ends of Earth. These days, I am encouraging my wife to tell her story, the process in which God brought her to help me to be completely free to love and to be loved.

If you, or anyone you know, can identify with my story, I want you to know there is hope. Prayer, fasting, intercession and above all, love, are the key to being triumphant. Don't falter, look for help. Don't give up, today God can make anyone free.

APPENDIX

What the Bible Tells Us

T HE BIBLE CLEARLY talks to us about the existence of demonic activity in human beings, even in believers. What I, as a person, can say on any matter is of relative importance. So, that is why, through the Word of God, I want to show the influence that the spiritual world has had, continues to have, and will have on the development of the human race and on the events that affect people's daily life until the end of time.

Be assured that it has taken me decades to arrive to this point in my life. Moreover, believing in all this was not easy. If I hadn't witnessed it first-hand, I wouldn't believe it. Even though I have seen some outstanding things, I tried to deny them due to the hardness of my heart and my deep desire for no one to deceive or manipulate me.

****

It is getting less and less common to discuss these matters in order to conform to this world, and I would be in the same position if it wasn't for what I experienced and suffered.

****

It is easier to keep quiet, to be politically correct and not to get involved in these matters, to avoid being branded a lunatic, a mad man, a crazy person, a sectarian, or a fanatic. It is getting less and less common to discuss these matters in order to conform to this world, and I would be in the same position if it wasn't for what I experienced and suffered. For this reason, I decided to tell part of my story in this book. As a Christian pastor, it is difficult for me to talk about these experiences. I imagine that many believers and brother pastors will be suffering the same internal struggle. Should we speak and risk being called a fanatic in the twenty-first century or should we keep quiet and stay on good terms with everyone?

Entering the spiritual realm can be something terrible if it hurts you and makes you suffer. Believing in these things in order to endure them is not a pleasant experience, but ignoring them also makes us easy prey for enemies disguised as angels of light.

Incredibly, the last book of the Bible talks to us about the origin of all the evil influences that exist on earth and of human ignorance. Below, I will show you some of the passages from the Bible that give us more clarity on this matter. I have not included them all, as there is a lot of material. However, I have included the most important and explanatory passages on the spiritual struggle for the body, soul, and spirit of human beings.

Everything Began in the Beginning

Satan was expelled from heaven, which is where he came from. Now, he is here on earth among us humans working to steal, kill, and destroy. He is accompanied by his demons and fallen angels.

> *The great dragon was hurled down—that ancient serpent called the devil, or Satan, who leads the whole world astray. He was hurled to the earth, and his angels with him.*
> Revelation 12:9, NVI®

The Intentions of the Enemy of Our Soul

The Bible clearly explains the purpose this evil being serves amongst us.

> *Be sober, be vigilant; because your adversary the devil walks about like a roaring lion, seeking whom he may devour.*
>
> 1 Peter 5:8

A Spiritual War of Worlds

These wicked spiritual entities hate what God loves most: human beings. They are permanently fighting against man and only want to put an end to him. This includes his peace, his enjoyment, his health, and his finances. They want to steal his peace and deprive him of any relationship with God.

> *For we do not wrestle against flesh and blood, but against principalities, against powers, against the rulers of the darkness of this age, against spiritual hosts of wickedness in the heavenly places.*
>
> Ephesians 6:12

Spiritual Arms

Believers in Jesus Christ have extremely powerful weapons available to them to help them to confront this evil world.

> *Put on the whole armor of God, that you may be able to stand against the wiles of the devil.*
>
> Ephesians 6:11

Believing in God is Not Enough

A distracted person may suppose that by simply believing in God they will be safe. However, a person's faith must be in action, in service. It is true that there is a war, and it is happening right now, at this precise moment while you are reading these lines and those who are caught off guard suffer more than those who are prepared.

> *You believe that there is one God? Good! Even the demons believe that—and shudder.*
> James 2:19, NVI®

Jesus, Our General in the Struggle

Jesus clearly showed his strategy in this spiritual war and expelled demons from human beings.

> *But if I cast out demons by the Spirit of God, surely the kingdom of God has come upon you.*
> Matthew 12:28

Jesus Commissioned the Apostles for This Struggle

With these words, we see that Jesus teaches the Apostles to expel demons.

> *Heal the sick, cleanse the lepers, raise the dead, cast out demons. Freely you have received, freely give.*
> Matthew 10:8

MARIO FERRO

Jesus Commissioned More People

In the following passage, Jesus commissioned seventy people to help in the spiritual struggle. This spiritual war is huge, including earth and the entire universe. The influence of the evil entities is absolute. Every man counts, every believer adds up and each one needs to do their part of the work.

The Church must be prepared and free in order to love and serve God. Our duty and our obligation is to be happy and to fill ourselves with the joy of the Lord. We must live productive and prosperous lives, showing the world how Christ lives within us. We can achieve this through good and harmonious marital relationships, the respect of children towards their parents in the family home, the protection and love of parents towards their children, taking care of our health and finances, thus glorifying our Lord. Integral prosperity is a demonstration that God lives in us. So, we have to do the work. That is why Jesus showed us the way.

> *Then the seventy returned with joy, saying, "Lord, even the demons are subject to us in Your name." And He said to them, "I saw Satan fall like lightning from heaven. Behold, I give you the authority to trample on serpents and scorpions, and over all the power of the enemy, and nothing shall by any means hurt you. Nevertheless do not rejoice in this, that the spirits are subject to you, but rather rejoice because your names are written in heaven.*
>
> Luke 10:17-20

Jesus Expelled the Demons From his Followers

Some women who walked with Christ were freed from these evil influences. For example, Mary Magdalene had seven demons in her.

> *Then Jesus rose early on the first day of the week,*
> *he appeared first to Mary Magdalene, out of whom*
> *he had driven seven demons.*
>
> Mark 16:9, NVI®

> *And also some women who had been cured of*
> *evil spirits and diseases: Mary (called Magdalene)*
> *from whom seven demons had come out.*
>
> Luke 8:2, NVI®

Recurrence

A human being can be completely free from demons. However, if their habits, confessions, friendships, attitudes, and faith do not change, it is likely that the plague in their house is worse than the previous one. In the Bible (New King James Version in the English translation), this passage is subtitled: "An Unclean Spirit Returns".

> *When an unclean spirit goes out of a man, he goes*
> *through dry places, seeking rest, and finds none.*
> *Then he says, 'I will return to my house from*
> *which I came.' And when he comes, he finds it*
> *empty, swept, and put in order. Then he goes and*
> *takes with him seven other spirits more wicked*
> *than himself, and they enter and dwell there; and*
> *the last state of that man is worse than the first. So*
> *shall it also be with this wicked generation.*
>
> Matthew 12:43-45

The Apostles Continued the Struggle

The spiritual struggle did not end when Jesus went to heaven. The Bible clearly states this. The Apostle Paul and his disciples continued to cast out demons.

> *Once when we were going to the place of prayer, we were met by a female slave who had a spirit by which she predicted the future. She earned a great deal of money for her owners by fortune-telling. She followed Paul and the rest of us, shouting,*
>
> *"These men are servants of the Most High God, who are telling you the way to be saved."*
>
> *She kept this up for many days. Finally Paul became so annoyed that he turned around and said to the spirit,*
>
> *"In the name of Jesus Christ I command you to come out of her!"*
>
> *At that moment the spirit left her.*
>
> *When her owners realized that their hope of making money was gone, they seized Paul and Silas and dragged them into the marketplace to face the authorities.*
>
> Acts 16:16-19, NVI®
>
> *Crowds gathered also from the towns around Jerusalem, bringing their sick and those tormented by impure spirits, and all of them were healed.*
>
> Acts 5:16, NVI®

The Final Days

As the Second Coming of the Lord Jesus Christ approaches, demonic activity will intensify.

> *They are demonic spirits that perform signs, and they go out to the kings of the whole world, to gather them for the battle on the great day of God Almighty.*
> Revelation 16:14, NVI®

Deceitful Spirits

Even believers will relent towards the end, because the influence of the world and these forces will be very strong. The fear of rejection and persecution will make many remain silent and even change the way they believe, think, and act.

> *Now the Spirit expressly says that in latter times some will depart from the faith, giving heed to deceiving spirits and doctrines of demons.*
> 1 Timothy 4:1

The End Will be Clear and Resounding

Jesus created His Church as a conquering entity, an invading force that, one day, must take possession of what He rescued through it and for it. We are not an insignificant little band of deluded, ignorant believers that are terrified of their enemy. On the contrary, we are powerful in God, we are strong in Christ, and we are the Church of Jesus.

And I say also unto thee, that thou art Peter, and upon this rock I will build my church; and the gates of hell shall not prevail against it.

Matthew 16:18, RVA

Because of Satan and His Demons

With these passages, I want to give you enough arguments and biblical evidence in order for you or someone you love to be set free and enjoy the life that God has given you on this Earth. Freedom is still possible and you have the opportunity to restore your faith and hope in God. Once you are free, through dedication, love and gratitude, you must spread this message to those who need it. There are many people who are sick, damaged, and tormented. However, the workers are still few. Nowadays, Satan can enter, possess, and influence people, animals, and things.

GENESIS

Because of a Demon... the Human Being Left God's Presence and Died

Now the serpent was more cunning than any beast of the field which the Lord God had made. And he said to the woman, "Has God indeed said, "You shall not eat of every tree of the garden'?" And the woman said to the serpent, "We may eat the fruit of the trees of the garden; but of the fruit of the tree which is in the midst of the garden, God has said, 'You shall not eat it, nor shall you touch it, lest you die.'" Then the serpent said to the woman, "You will not surely die. For God knows that in the day you eat of it your eyes will be opened, and you will be like God, knowing good and evil." So when the woman saw that the tree was good for food, that it was pleasant to the eyes, and a tree desirable to make one wise, she took of its fruit and ate. She also gave to her husband with her, and he ate. Then the eyes of both of them were opened, and they knew that they were naked; and they sewed fig leaves together and made themselves coverings.

And they heard the sound of the Lord God walking in the garden in the cool of the day, and the man and his wife hid themselves from the presence of the Lord God among the trees of the garden. Then the Lord God called to the man and said to him, "Where are you?" So he said, "I heard Your voice in the garden, and I was afraid because I was naked; and I hid myself." And He said, "Who told you that you were naked? Have you eaten from the tree of which I commanded you that you should not eat?" Then the man said, "The woman whom You gave to be with me, she gave me of the tree, and I ate." And the Lord God said to the woman, "What is this you have done?" The woman said, "The serpent deceived me, and I ate." So the Lord God said to the serpent: "Because you have done this, you are cursed more than all cattle and more than every beast of the field; on your belly you shall go and you shall eat dust all the days of your life.

Genesis 3:1-14

MATTHEW

Because of a Demon... Two Men Acted Like Wild Animals

When He had come to the other side, to the country of the Gergesenes, there met Him two

MARIO FERRO

demon-possessed men, coming out of the tombs, exceedingly fierce, so that no one could pass that way. And suddenly they cried out, saying, "What have we to do with You, Jesus, You Son of God? Have You come here to torment us before the time?" Now a good way off from them there was a herd of many swine feeding. So the demons begged Him, saying, "If You cast us out, permit us to go away into the herd of swine." And He said to them, "Go." So when they had come out, they went into the herd of swine. And suddenly the whole herd of swine ran violently down the steep place into the sea, and perished in the water. Then those who kept them fled; and they went away into the city and told everything, including what had happened to the demon-possessed men. And behold, the whole city came out to meet Jesus. And when they saw Him, they begged Him to depart from their region.

Matthew 8:28-34

Because of a Demon...A Man was Mute

As they went out, behold, they brought to Him a man, mute and demon-possessed. And when the demon was cast out, the mute spoke. And the multitudes marveled, saying, "It was never seen like this in Israel!" But the Pharisees said, "He casts out demons by the ruler of the demons."

Matthew 9:32-34

Because of a Demon... Jesus Disciplines the Apostle Peter

But He turned and said to Peter, "Get behind Me, Satan! You are an offense to Me, for you are

not mindful of the things of God, but the things
of men."

Matthew 16:23

MARK

Because of a Demon... Jesus is Tempted

> *Immediately the Spirit drove Him into the*
> *wilderness. And He was there in the wilderness*
> *forty days, tempted by Satan, and was with the*
> *wild beasts; and the angels ministered to Him.*

Mark 1:12-13

Because of a Demon...A Man is Possessed

> *Then they went into Capernaum, and immediately*
> *on the Sabbath He entered the synagogue and*
> *taught. And they were astonished at His teaching,*
> *for He taught them as one having authority, and*
> *not as the scribes.*
>
> *Now there was a man in their synagogue with*
> *an unclean spirit. And he cried out, saying, "Let*
> *us alone! What have we to do with You, Jesus of*
> *Nazareth? Did You come to destroy us? I know*
> *who You are the Holy One of God!"*
>
> *But Jesus rebuked him, saying, "Be quiet, and*
> *come out of him!" And when the unclean spirit*
> *had convulsed him and cried out with a loud voice,*
> *he came out of him. Then they were all amazed,*
> *so that they questioned among themselves, saying,*
> *"What is this? What new doctrine is this? For with*
> *authority He commands even the unclean spirits,*

*and they obey Him." And immediately His fame
spread throughout all the region around Galilee.*

Mark 1:21-28

Because of a Demon... Multitudes were Sick and Possessed

*At evening, when the sun had set, they brought to
Him all who were sick and those who were demon-
possessed. And the whole city was gathered together
at the door. Then He healed many who were sick
with various diseases, and cast out many demons;
and He did not allow the demons to speak, because
they knew Him.*

Mark 1:32-34

Because of a Demon... A Young Man Wanted to Kill Himself

*And when He came to the disciples, He saw a great
multitude around them, and scribes disputing
with them. Immediately, when they saw Him,
all the people were greatly amazed, and running
to Him, greeted Him. And He asked the scribes,
"What are you discussing with them?" Then one of
the crowd answered and said, "Teacher, I brought
You my son, who has a mute spirit. And wherever
it seizes him, it throws him down; he foams at
the mouth, gnashes his teeth, and becomes rigid.
So I spoke to Your disciples, that they should cast
it out, but they could not." He answered him and
said, "O faithless generation, how long shall I be
with you? How long shall I bear with you? Bring
him to Me." Then they brought him to Him.
And when he saw Him, immediately the spirit
convulsed him, and he fell on the ground and
wallowed, foaming at the mouth. So He asked
his father, "How long has this been happening to*

him?" And he said, "From childhood. And often he has thrown him both into the fire and into the water to destroy him. But if You can do anything, have compassion on us and help us." Jesus said to him, "If you can believe, all things are possible to him who believes." Immediately the father of the child cried out and said with tears, "Lord, I believe; help my unbelief!" When Jesus saw that the people came running together, He rebuked the unclean spirit, saying to it: "Deaf and dumb spirit, I command you, come out of him and enter him no more!" Then the spirit cried out, convulsed him greatly, and came out of him. And he became as one dead, so that many said, "He is dead." But Jesus took him by the hand and lifted him up, and he arose. And when He had come into the house, His disciples asked Him privately, "Why could we not cast it out?" So He said to them, "This kind can come out by nothing but prayer and fasting."

Mark 9:14-29

LUKE

Because of a Demon... Multitudes Were Tormented and Sick

And He came down with them and stood on a level place with a crowd of His disciples and a great multitude of people from all Judea and Jerusalem, and from the seacoast of Tyre and Sidon, who came to hear Him and be healed of their diseases, as well as those who were tormented with unclean spirits. And they were healed. And the whole multitude sought to touch Him, for power went out from Him and healed them all.

Luke 6:17-19

Because of a Demon... Jesus Showed us the Complete Strategy

And He was casting out a demon, and it was mute. So it was, when the demon had gone out, that the mute spoke; and the multitudes marveled. But some of them said, "He casts out demons by Beelzebub, the ruler of the demons." Others, testing Him, sought from Him a sign from heaven. But He, knowing their thoughts, said to them: "Every kingdom divided against itself is brought to desolation, and a house divided against a house falls. If Satan also is divided against himself, how will his kingdom stand? Because you say I cast out demons by Beelzebub. And if I cast out demons by Beelzebub, by whom do your sons cast them out? Therefore they will be your judges. But if I cast out demons with the finger of God, surely the kingdom of God has come upon you. When a strong man, fully armed, guards his own palace, his goods are in peace. But when a stronger than he comes upon him and overcomes him, he takes from him all his armor in which he trusted, and divides his spoils. He who is not with Me is against Me, and he who does not gather with Me scatters. When an unclean spirit goes out of a man, he goes through dry places, seeking rest; and finding none, he says, 'I will return to my house from which I came.' And when he comes, he finds it swept and put in order. Then he goes and takes with him seven other spirits more wicked than himself, and they enter and dwell there; and the last state of that man is worse than the first.

Luke 11:14-26

JOHN

Because of a Demon... Judas Betrays Jesus

> When Jesus had said these things, He was troubled
> in spirit, and testified and said, "Most assuredly,
> I say to you, one of you will betray Me." Then
> the disciples looked at one another, perplexed
> about whom He spoke. Now there was leaning
> on Jesus' bosom one of His disciples, whom Jesus
> loved. Simon Peter therefore motioned to him to
> ask who it was of whom He spoke. Then, leaning
> back[a] on Jesus' breast, he said to Him, "Lord,
> who is it?" Jesus answered, "It is he to whom I
> shall give a piece of bread when I have dipped it."
> And having dipped the bread, He gave it to Judas
> Iscariot, the son of Simon. Now after the piece of
> bread, Satan entered him. Then Jesus said to him,
> "What you do, do quickly." But no one at the table
> knew for what reason He said this to him. For
> some thought, because Judas had the money box,
> that Jesus had said to him, "Buy those things we
> need for the feast," or that he should give something
> to the poor. Having received the piece of bread,
> he then went out immediately. And it was night.
>
> John 13:21-30

Free Through God's Love

As you can see in the previous passages, the struggle is
tenacious and persistent. God loves his creation, but what
He loves most are human beings. The passage which is most
repeated by believers says:

For God so loved the world that He gave His only begotten Son, that whoever believes in Him should not perish but have everlasting life.

John 3:16

In other words, God loved humanity so much that he delivered Jesus to rescue it. God gave His only Son and Himself for you and me, so that one day we can return to his presence and live at His side forever.

All those who believe in Jesus and confess Him as their Savior and Lord, will receive this eternal present. However, while they live on this earth, they will be able to enjoy the advantages of being free and prospering in everything they propose in accordance to the will of God.

I am living testimony of a life that has been renewed, changed and transformed for the glory of God. Even though I lost some years due to ignorance, obstinacy, stubbornness and spiritual blindness, God used my toughness to help many others, who, today, through my change, can glorify His name and follow only Him. I am a walking, talking and breathing testimony that proves that, no matter the circumstances in which a human lives, God wants to help you and give you the strength to overcome it. We are united with Him for eternity.

ABOUT THE AUTHOR

MARIO FERRO, BORN in Bogota, Colombia, studied acting in the Bogota School of Dramatic Arts. He was a professional, street, theater, and radio actor. He appeared in countless soap operas and television series. He was also a leading actor for fifteen years. One day he was introduced to the Gospel by Nelly Moreno, one of the country's most popular actresses, who is now his wife. Mario and Nelly are the parents of three children: Daniela, David, and Camila. His life radically changed once he learned about Jesus Christ and Mario embraced his faith. His decisions through Jesus led him to abandon acting, which had been his passion until that moment. However, Jesus gave him a true purpose in life and from that moment, he served in his local church as an evangelist and founded the WWJD Ministry, named after the initials of the words *Walking With Jesus Daily*. He later travelled to Miami, Florida, where he is now based and pastors a church of the same name.

WWJD IS AN international ministry dedicated to spreading the gospel through its discipleship, fulfilling the Lord Jesus Christ's command to go out to the whole world making disciples.

With headquarters in the United States and Colombia, the WWJD ministry, named after the initials of the words *Walking With Jesus Daily,* was founded more than eighteen years ago by Mario Ferro and Nelly Moreno. The ministry is focused on the transformation of individuals through new birth, walking with each person daily, knowing their struggles, their origins and forgiveness, in order to bring about change for the service of the Kingdom.

Even after knowing the truth of the gospel, humans can continue to feel that they have no purpose and can go through very dark moments. Being able to count on someone at that time can be a determining factor in a Christian's growth. It is also of invaluable help to have a mentor, a leader, a discipler, or a teacher. The ministry is aware of this and has proposed to make sure that every believer has someone in their life until they develop and become a leader who, in turn, will help others going through their own process.

WWJD is in a phase of expansion, since the years spent sowing in the life of its leaders have begun to pay off and we can see how the ministry is spreading to other cities and countries. Every member of the flock that travels for various reasons, wishes for a WWJD church in their place of work. This is why we understand that the training of leaders is fundamental in the development of any ministry. We are not only referring to growth in numbers, but also to having the real basis for true growth. Sometimes, the work seems slow, but with patience and time, everything sowed gives its fruits.

For eighteen years this work was silently undertaken, but today, the day has arrived to go out to work more energetically. The world is changing quickly and radically. So, this is when the work of the true Church of Jesus Christ should be seen. Mayor Luigi Boria highlights this when he says that "our city feels blessed by the spiritual support and help given by Pastor Mario in Doral and in other communities [...], and that is why I think that Mario Ferro and his wife, Nelly, are doing an excellent job."

There is hope that we will overcome our problems and that is why we must fulfill our mission to let the world see the light that must shine in the middle of the darkness. This is what we dedicate our lives to and will continue to do so with the help of our good Lord.

Mario at age 5

Grandfather Luis and Mario's cousin.

Mario at 19 when he was already a model.

Mario at age 20 while he acted in a Colombian soap opera.

Nelly Moreno when she met Mario, her-now husband.

Mario and Nelly's wedding.

Mario and Nelly now.

<barcode>||| ||| ||| ||| ||| ||| || ||| ||| ||| || ||| ||| |||</barcode>

Printed in the United States
By Bookmasters